ANSWER KEY

French for Children

Primer A

Learn more than how to order a croissant

Joshua Kraut, PhD
with David Spieser, PhD

French for Children Primer A Answer Key
© Classical Academic Press, 2015
Version 1.1

ISBN: 978-1-60051-280-3

All rights reserved. This publication may not be reproduced,
stored in a retrieval system, or transmitted, in any form or by any means,
without the prior written permission of Classical Academic Press.

Classical Academic Press
515 S. 32nd Street
Camp Hill, PA 17011

www.ClassicalAcademicPress.com

Illustrations by Jason Rayner
Book design by Lauraine Gustafson

Notebook image courtesy of designious/Vecteezy.com
Ladder image courtesy of freevector/Vecteezy.com

TABLE OF CONTENTS

Title	Page
CD Track & Audio File Information	vi
Suggested Schedule	1
Introduction	5
Pronunciation Wizard	9

Partie	Chapitre	Chant	Grammar Topics	Page
1	1	**Je parle** (I speak, I am speaking)	Verbs	25
	2	**Parler** (to speak/talk)	Subjects; Verbs: Number; Verbs: Person	35
	3	**Finir** (to finish)	Verb Endings; Infinitives; **Faux Amis**	46
	4	Subject Pronouns	Subject Pronouns vs. Subjects; Hidden Mysteries of Pronouns, Part 1	59
	5	REVIEW	REVIEW; Hidden Mysteries of Pronouns, Part 2	73
2	6	**Le** and **La** (The)	Nouns; Gender	82
	7	Gender	Articles; Subject Pronouns; Hidden Mysteries of Pronouns, Part 3	93
	8	**J'ai, Avoir** (I have, to have)	Irregular Verbs, Part 1: **Avoir**; **Un/Une** and **Des**; Definite and Indefinite Articles	104
	9	Plurals	Tricky Plurals; The Curious Haves, Part 1	117
	10	REVIEW	REVIEW	126
3	11	The Forms of **De**	The Daring **De**; The Curious Haves, Part 2	134
	12	**Un chien sympathique** (A nice dog)	Adjectives; Word Order Using Adjectives; The Curious Haves, Part 3	143
	13	**Amusant, amusants** (Funny)	Adjective Agreement	153
	14	**Bon et beau** (Good and beautiful)	BAGS Adjectives; Three Tricky Feminine Adjectives; The Curious Haves, Part 4	168
	15	**Mon, ma, mes** (My)	Possessive Adjectives	179
	16	REVIEW	REVIEW	191
	17	END-OF-BOOK REVIEW	REVIEW	198

Title	Page
Vocabulaire by Chapter	205
Alphabetical **Vocabulaire**	213
Categorical **Vocabulaire**	219
Appendix A: Dialogue Translations	226
Appendix B: Chant Translations	240
Appendix C: Prepositions	244
Appendix D: Verbs	245

CD Track & Audio File Information

CD Track	Audio File	Chap.	Page	CD Track	Audio File	Chap.	Page	CD Track	Audio File	Chap.	Page
1	0PW_01	PW	9	39	03_05	3	58	77	12_03	12	144
2	0PW_02	PW	11	40	04_01	4	59	78	12_04	12	144
3	0PW_03	PW	12	41	04_02	4	60	79	12_05	12	152
4	0PW_04	PW	13	42	04_03	4	60	80	13_01	13	153
5	0PW_05	PW	14	43	04_04	4	60	81	13_02	13	153
6	0PW_06	PW	15	44	04_05	4	72	82	13_03	13	154
7	0PW_07	PW	15	45	05_01	5	80	83	13_04	13	154
8	0PW_08	PW	16	46	06_01	6	82	84	13_05	13	156
9	0PW_09	PW	16	47	06_02	6	82	85	13_06	13	160
10	0PW_10	PW	17	48	06_03	6	83	86	13_07	13	167
11	0PW_11	PW	17	49	06_04	6	83	87	14_01	14	168
12	0PW_12	PW	17	50	06_05	6	92	88	14_02	14	169
13	0PW_13	PW	17	51	07_01	7	93	89	14_03	14	169
14	0PW_14	PW	18	52	07_02	7	94	90	14_04	14	169
15	0PW_15	PW	19	53	07_03	7	94	91	14_05	14	174
16	0PW_16	PW	19	54	07_04	7	95	92	14_06	14	178
17	0PW_17	PW	20	55	07_05	7	100	93	15_01	15	179
18	0PW_18	PW	20	56	07_06	7	103	94	15_02	15	180
19	0PW_19	PW	20	57	08_01	8	104	95	15_03	15	180
20	0PW_20	PW	21	58	08_02	8	105	96	15_04	15	181
21	0PW_21	PW	21	59	08_03	8	105	97	15_05	15	190
22	0PW_22	PW	21	60	08_04	8	105				
23	0PW_23	PW	22	61	08_05	8	116				
24	0PW_24	PW	23	62	09_01	9	117				
25	01_01	1	25	63	09_02	9	117				
26	01_02	1	26	64	09_03	9	118				
27	01_03	1	26	65	09_04	9	118				
28	01_04	1	26	66	09_05	9	119				
29	01_05	1	34	67	09_06	9	120				
30	02_01	2	35	68	09_07	9	125				
31	02_02	2	36	69	10_01	10	133				
32	02_03	2	36	70	11_01	11	134				
33	02_04	2	37	71	11_02	11	135				
34	02_05	2	45	72	11_03	11	135				
35	03_01	3	46	73	11_04	11	135				
36	03_02	3	47	74	11_05	11	142				
37	03_03	3	47	75	12_01	12	143				
38	03_04	3	48	76	12_02	12	144				

⚜ SUGGESTED SCHEDULE ⚜

There are seventeen chapters in *French for Children Primer A*, of which thirteen are content chapters and four are review. Doing one chapter per week (content and review chapters) will allow you to finish the course in approximately half of an academic year. Alternatively, if you complete one content chapter every two weeks, taking just one week per review chapter, the course will take a full year—thirty weeks.

Weekly Schedule

The following is a basic weekly schedule, to be modified as necessary by the teacher. Note that days two and five call for longer sessions.

Day One (approx. 30 mins.)

Listen to the audio file of the opening dialogue and have students follow along in the text. Take a few minutes (not too long) to ask students what they've understood from the dialogue and what they think is going on. Comprehension at this stage may be very minimal, but students should be encouraged to guess at details of the plot or simply the meaning of a single word. Present the vocabulary and the paradigm (grammar chant). Students should chant through the paradigm and vocabulary two or three times, using the recorded audio files (and/or teachers' pronunciation) as a guide. (Optional step 1: At this point, the video can be played up to the point at which the instructor reads through the chant and the vocabulary, but the video should be stopped after that.) Then, ask students to skim back over the dialogue to see if they understand more of the French. Again, do not take too long for comprehension questions at this stage; the dialogue will be revisited later. (Optional step 2: Students can take turns reading different parts in the dialogue, one or two lines each. This activity is meant to help students read the French and develop good French pronunciation more than to stage a drama, since comprehension may still be minimal.)

Day Two (approx. 55–65 mins.)

Review the paradigm (grammar chant) and vocabulary and have students chant them again one or two times. Watch the video (either picking up where you left off from day one or viewing it in its entirety). The videos are approximately forty-five minutes to an hour in length. While you should feel free to stop them and rewind at any time, be aware that they may take a while to get through with frequent interruptions.

Day Three (approx. 30 mins.)

Start with a quick chant of the paradigm and vocabulary. Then spend some time explaining the grammar page, paying special attention to the examples. If you see an italicized sentence, be sure to emphasize it (you may consider having students circle these and other key sentences with a colored pencil for future reference). Ask comprehension questions, such as "Can you tell me how a French adjective is different from an English adjective?" or "What is a pronoun?" After this, begin the worksheet, or assign it as homework.

Day Four (approx. 30 mins.)

Again, start the day with a quick chant of the paradigm and vocabulary. Next, the worksheet should either be started or completed. Check students' work and go over any corrections with the students. Grammar should be reviewed and retaught as necessary. One means of reviewing grammar can be to view the video again to ensure comprehension of key grammatical topics for that chapter.

Day Five (approx. 50 mins.)

Students should take the quiz without looking back at the rest of the chapter. When the quiz has been completed, go over the answers together and review any trouble spots. Finally, go back and listen to the opening dialogue once more, having students follow along in the text. Discuss what is happening, and identify vocabulary/grammatical points that help you understand the dialogue. Translate the dialogue together.

Biweekly Schedule

The following is a basic biweekly schedule spread over seven class meetings, to be modified as necessary by the teacher.

Day One (approx. 30 mins.)

Listen to the opening dialogue and follow along in the text. Take a few minutes (not too long) to ask students what they've understood from the dialogue, and what they think is going on. Comprehension at this stage may be very minimal, but students should be encouraged to guess at details of the plot or simply the meaning of a single word. Present the vocabulary and the paradigm (grammar chant). Students should chant through the paradigm and vocabulary two or three times, using the recorded audio files (and/or teachers' pronunciation) as a guide. (Optional step 1: At this point, the video can be played up to the point at which the instructor reads through the chant and the vocabulary, but it should be stopped after that.) Then, ask students to skim back over the dialogue to see if they understand more of the French. Again, do not take too long for comprehension questions at this stage; the dialogue will be revisited later. (Optional step 2: Students can take turns reading different parts in the dialogue, one or two lines each. This activity is meant to help students read and develop good French pronunciation more than to stage a drama, since comprehension may still be minimal.

Day Two (approx. 55–65 mins.)

Review the paradigm (grammar chant) and vocabulary and have students chant them again one or two times. Have students watch the video (either picking up where you left off from day one, or else in its entirety). The videos are between forty-five minutes and an hour in length. While you should feel free to stop them and rewind at any time, be aware that they may take a while to get through with frequent interruptions.

Day Three (approx. 30 mins.)

Start with a quick chant of the paradigm and vocabulary. Then spend some time explaining the grammar page, paying special attention to the examples. If you see an italicized sentence, be sure to emphasize it (you may consider having students circle or highlight these and other key sentences for future reference). Ask comprehension questions, such as "Can you tell me how a French adjective is different from an English adjective?" or "What is a pronoun?" Go back and listen to the opening dialogue once more, having students follow along in the text. Discuss what is happening, and identify vocabulary/grammatical points that help you understand the dialogue (a full translation is not necessary at this time—target in particular those sections of the dialogue that employ grammatical notions discussed in the Grammar section). If time remains, have students begin the worksheet.

Day Four (approx. 30 mins.)

Again, start the day with a quick chant of the paradigm and vocabulary. Next, the worksheet should be started. Students may consult the chapter to complete this section. Grammar should be reviewed and retaught as necessary. One means of reviewing grammar can be to view parts of the video again to ensure comprehension of key grammatical topics for that chapter.

Day Five (approx. 30 mins.)

The worksheet should be completed and reviewed. Trouble spots should be addressed. Students should prepare for taking the quiz by playing vocabulary games (e.g., flash cards, bingo, charades, etc.).

Day Six (approx. 30 mins.)

Have students take the quiz, noting that they are not to look back at the previous sections of the chapter.

Day Seven (approx. 30 mins.)

Review the quiz. Then, return a final time to the opening dialogue, having students listen to the audio file and follow along in the text. Translate the dialogue together. Discuss what is happening and identify vocabulary/grammatical points that help you understand the dialogue. Students may be encouraged to read aloud and to do their best to "act the part" if they feel so inclined.

INTRODUCTION

Before beginning our first lesson, let's talk about how this book works. The first thing you'll encounter after this introduction is the Pronunciation Wizard. This fairly self-explanatory wizard will be used over the course of the first few chapters. It is first mentioned in the Worksheet section of chapter 1. Even after you've finished with it (in chapter 5), feel free to flip back to it or listen again to the audio files for any questions you may have about the wonderful world of French pronunciation.

After the Pronunciation Wizard, you'll find the actual chapters of the book. There are two types of chapters: *lesson chapters* and *review chapters*. Review chapters are the easiest to explain. They simply bring together the information you've seen in the previous few chapters and give you an opportunity to test your knowledge. Lesson chapters, then, are where you learn things for the first time.

In each lesson chapter, you will see a few things: At the top of each page in the lesson chapters, you will see different titles. The title that is BIGGER THAN THE REST tells you which part of a chapter you are in. The four main parts of each lesson chapter are: Memory, Grammar, Worksheet, and Quiz. Let's take a look at what you'll find in each of the different parts.

MEMORY

Dialogue:

The dialogues in this book weave together a somewhat peculiar story. Without revealing too much here in the introduction, we shall simply say that they relate the adventures of two four-legged companions of considerably different sizes and their meetings with other animals, as well as occasional people, whom they encounter along their way.

The *Fables* of Jean de La Fontaine, if you know them, may come to mind as you read through the dialogues—not every dialogue, but a good number of them. Many of these fables have an even earlier author with whom you may be familiar: the Greek poet, Aesop. A number of Aesop's fables were adapted by La Fontaine (in French, of course) almost 2,000 years after they were originally written!

More practically, the dialogues introduce you to some of the new vocabulary that you'll be learning in each chapter. Feel free to read over the chapter's vocabulary list before reading the dialogue if you desire, but we do not recommend that you try to memorize it letter-for-letter before attempting to read the dialogues.

In fact, the most rewarding way to approach the dialogues may simply be to *jump right in and try to figure out what words mean by their context.* You will often see a mix of French and English in the dialogues—especially at the beginning of the book—which should help you understand the context of the conversation better. In many cases, this mixture of languages should also make it possible for you to decipher the new French words in each chapter. Even if you can only narrow it down to a guess (for example: "I think this word must be some kind of food," or "I think this word is an action that means to go somewhere"), that's a great start. This will give you a "feel" for the word even before you study the vocabulary more deeply.

Chant:

The French word **chant** means the same thing as the English word "chant," so you already know a French word! In each chapter we ask you to chant a certain set of words or phrases. Why? The goal is to help you and your mouth get used to forming the sounds of these words. You can listen to the audio files of the chants, which will also help you to learn how to pronounce them correctly.

Vocabulaire:

There are approximately ten vocabulary words in each chapter. After reading through the dialogue and trying to figure out the new words ahead of time, we recommend that you spend a few minutes committing these words to memory every day that you are working on the chapter. Memorize the vocabulary, and the chapter will be easy as pie to follow. Don't memorize it, and you'll be flipping pages back and forth the whole time to look up what the words mean! Try making flash cards and having someone quiz you.

Grammar

This section is where we discuss the inner workings of French grammar—and how to use it. Pay close attention to a few different *icons* that may appear on the pages of the Grammar section:

 Remarque: The French word **remarque** looks like an English word you may know—"remark." In this book, when you see the **Remarque** icon, this means that you will be given a little bit of extra information to remember about the grammar rule you've just learned.

Renvoi: A **renvoi** is a sort of reminder to go back to a subject that has already been mentioned. For example, if we are talking about something in chapter 16, which uses some of the information from chapter 7, there will be a **Renvoi** icon in chapter 16, which tells you "turn to chapter 7 if you need to refresh your memory."

Worksheet

The Worksheet is just what the name says it is: worksheet exercises where you can put your brain to the test and see if you can use the grammar lesson to complete the charts, sentences, and word puzzles you'll find. For the Worksheet, feel free to flip back and forth between the exercises and the pages in the Grammar section in case you get stuck; the idea is to learn as you go. (Answers to the exercises from both the Worksheet and the Quiz section are found in *French for Children Primer A Answer Key*.)

Quiz

Finally, the end of each lesson chapter contains a Quiz section. This section is similar to the Worksheet, except this time you're *only* supposed to use your brain—no looking back at the Grammar section, the Worksheet, your flash cards, your notes, nothing, zero, zip, **rien** (**rien** is French for "nothing"). Of course, **la police** won't come to your house if you do go back and look, but the point is that *if you still need to go back to previous pages for help, you have not really learned the lesson*, and so you should probably not go on to the next chapter until you can pass the quiz with either a perfect score or only one or two incorrect answers. And, of course, once you're done with the quiz, we highly recommend going back to the opening dialogue and reading it through once more—probably much faster, and more enjoyably this time!—to cement in all of the new things you've learned.

La dictée:

At the end of every Quiz section we've included an exercise called a **dictée**—a dictation. Traditionally in this type of exercise the teacher reads a short sentence slowly, a few words at a time, and the students copy down, or transcribe, what they hear. For each chapter, you may want to play the **dictée** CD track/audio file so that students can hear the sentences read aloud and then, if you're comfortable doing so, read the sentences aloud yourself, including perhaps a faster repetition (one which approaches a normal speech rate) the second time.

Transcribing spoken French is especially helpful since, as you'll see, there are many letters that may not be pronounced, but which are important to include in the written form nonetheless. The **dictée** has a rich tradition in francophone culture—a bit like our spelling bees. There are **dictée** competitions in many different francophone regions and they attract both schoolchildren and adults! Our hope is that these "spoken puzzles" will be challenging and instructive for you as well.

Treasures in the Back of the Book

Far, far away, in the back of this book, you will find several things:

Appendices:

The appendices contain some of the same information you will learn from the book's regular lesson chapters, but condensed and organized into charts to make it easier to search through. You'll find dialogue and chant translations in the first two appendices and a preposition appendix (appendix C; prepositions appear throughout the book). There is a verb appendix (appendix D) with verb conjugations (see chapter 3).

Glossaries:

The alphabetical glossary contains all of the vocabulary items in this book, along with their translations, presented in one long, alphabetical list. Think of this section as a "mini dictionary" just for the words of this book. For nouns, you will see the clues to determining the noun's gender (see chapter 6) in the glossary entry. In the glossary by chapter, you guessed it, all of the vocabulary words are listed by the chapter in which they first appear. This glossary can be a very handy tool when you're studying your vocabulary.

TEACHER'S NOTE

A few practical tips: First, you should feel free to incorporate the **dictées** in the Worksheet section (rather than the Quiz section) if you find that more helpful or if it works more neatly with your schedule. Second, as for the marking of the **dictées** (assuming they are being used in a Quiz), you should be generous with "partial credit" in these exercises. It can be quite challenging to get the entire sentence exactly right, so having a breakdown of how students can obtain points for each sentence—rather using an all-or-nothing scheme—would be preferable. One could award points, for example, for each correctly spelled word.

Pronunciation Wizard

Introduction

Welcome to the Pronunciation Wizard! This section of the book is designed to help you (and your mouth) get ready for some of the tricky new sounds of the French language. Remember one thing as you wander through all of the information in this section: *The letters that you see on the page are only hints for how to say each word.* What does this mean? Why are we just giving you hints, and not the *real thing*? What kind of book is this? Well, actually we are giving you both the hints and the real thing: There are audio files for this book that have lots of different recordings of French, both for this Pronunciation Wizard and for the chapters that follow. As you go through this Pronunciation Wizard, you should listen to the audio files that are associated with it (they are labeled with "0PW" and then a number) so you can hear the *true sound* of each word. *That* is what you want to sound like when you speak. We tell you which audio file to listen to for each new sound as you explore this wizard, so don't worry about losing your place.

At the beginning of the section, we just give you separate *words* to listen to and then repeat. For example, you might have: 1. **chat** 2. **chez** 3. **chameau** (0PW_01/Tr. 1). You can try to pronounce these words by yourself first, and then check yourself with the audio file—or you can just listen to the audio file first and then try to imitate the sounds you hear for each word.

About halfway through this wizard, we start giving you *whole sentences* to listen to (and repeat, if you dare!). In these cases, only the "new" words are numbered—that is, only the words with the new sound we're working on in that section of the Pronunciation Wizard will have the little number next to them. So for example, one of the sentences you'll encounter later in this wizard is:

Le roi[1] **René**[2] **est enrhumé**[3]!
King René has a cold!

In this case, we'll be working on the *r* sound, so only words with an *r* in them are numbered. Be sure to pay special attention to the numbered words since they contain the sound we're working on in each example.

French pronunciation can be tricky, but it's not **impossible**. Your mouth is the exact same kind of mouth that French speakers have—you just need to learn to use it like they use theirs! So, here is some final advice: Think of your ears as very high-tech microphones that can record every detail of every sound. As you listen to the pronunciation audio files, "record" all of the sounds you hear. Then, imagine what your mouth (and your throat and lips) need to do to reproduce the exact same sound you heard, and "replay" the sound with your own voice. Do this even if you think you sound a little strange. Because "strange" is exactly how you need to sound when you speak a foreign language—it's different from your language, after all!

By the way, do you know how to say "strange" in French? It's **étrange**. And guess how you say "foreign language" in French? It's **langue étrangère** (strange language).

Voilà, *a famous French proverb: "Impossible is not French!" Another way we might say it is, "Impossible is not a French word!"*

Une toute petite première leçon (A Little Tiny First Lesson)

Say the word "through" in English. How did you pronounce it? Did you say, "THREW-GUH-HUH"? No? Why not? Look at all of those letters! The *g* and the *h* at the end of the word can't just do *nothing*, can they? Of course they can. There are many English words that do not use all of the letters they have. Can you think of any more words that don't use all of their letters? What about: "debt," "ghost," "whistle," and "although"? We sure hope you don't say DE-BUH-T, GUH-HOST, WUH-HIS-TULL, and ALTHOU-GUH-HUH. If you do, forget about French—go work on your English!

Why do so many English words have "unnecessary" letters? That's a fair question. One of the main reasons for this curious overload of letters is the fact that these words *used to be* pronounced with all of the sounds intact. Does that mean that English speakers used to say things like THREW-GUH-HUH for "through"? Well, not necessarily: Since many of our English words come from other languages (and other countries), some of these old pronunciations actually may never have been used by *English* speakers.

Either way, over the course of time (many hundreds of years), people have found ways to pronounce these words without going to the trouble of saying each letter. But the way we write and spell words can never quite keep up with the way we say them, so we are often left with "old-looking" words that contain "extra" letters. While this can be confusing sometimes, think of how neat it is to be able to see how people hundreds of years ago, in distant lands, were pronouncing some of the same words we still use today!

Why are we talking about this? Because French has lots, heaps, tons, oodles, *thousands* of words whose letters are not all pronounced. The first lesson of the Pronunciation Wizard, then, is *be careful not to say too much*! Here are a few examples of French words:

Mon[1] **chat**[2]   **dort**[3]   **toujours**[4].
My   cat   sleeps   all the time (always).

Now listen to the audio file (0PW_02/Tr. 2: Pronunciation, Part A).

What's missing from the pronunciation of these words? Write down the letters of the sounds that are missing from the four words in that sentence.

1. _n_   2. _t_   3. _t_   4. _s_

If you wrote down: 1. **n**, 2. **t** 3. **t** and 4. **s**, you got it! That means that, if you actually *said*, "**MoN chaT dorT toujourS**," pronouncing all of the letters, you would have said *too much*! A French speaker might not have understood you.

Mon is pronounced MO; **chat** is pronounced SHA; **dort** is pronounced like "door"; and **toujours** is pronounced TOO-[3]OOR (where the [3] is like the *s* in "measure" or "pleasure").

Now, with our first lesson (Shhh! Don't say too much!) behind us, let's look at the French alphabet. The best way to learn the names of the letters is to sing them, so listen to the audio file (0PW_03/Tr. 3, you'll probably recognize the tune) and follow along with the letters:

A B C D E F G H I J K L M N O P Q R S T U V W X Y et Z, maintenant je sais mon alphabet, prochaine fois, chante avec moi! (The end of the French version goes, "... now I know my alphabet, next time sing with me!")

Practice saying the names of the letters a few times with the song on the audio file, stopping it and starting it as needed. The tricky ones to remember for us English speakers are usually the letters **G** and **J**, since they sound almost the opposite in French (in other words, the French **G** sounds much like the English *J* and the French **J** sounds much like the English *G*). The French **Y** can also be tough to remember. It's actually the words **i-grec**, which in English means "Greek *i*."

Vowels

Now, take a look at the French vowels:

a e i o u and sometimes **y**

Wait a minute: They're the same as English vowels! That was easy! Not so fast, Mr. or Ms. French-Is-a-Piece-of-Cake. Just think about English vowels for a second. Think about, say, the letter *a* and how it's pronounced in the following words: "ball," "band," "bay."

Enjoy fun practice at www.HeadventureLand.com!

All of these words contain the letter *a*. However, none of the *a*'s make the same sound! Why? The letter *a* makes different sounds in English depending on its neighboring letters. That's right: One little letter (*a*) has just made *three* different sounds. So, if English vowels can make different sounds when their neighboring letters change, it stands to reason that French vowels can, too. Now take a look at the French vowels again, and try to guess how many different sounds they can make:

1. **a**   2. **e**   3. **i**   4. **o**   5. **u** and sometimes   6. **y** can make: ____ sounds.

Now, look at the next page.

Did you guess *sixteen* different sounds? That is the real number. Let's see how these sounds actually work.

Listen closely to the audio files in the following sections to hear how these vowels should be pronounced. For each French vowel, we try to offer you the English version of the sound, but honestly, some of the French sounds have no equivalent in English. This means you have to make your mouth produce something *new* and maybe even a little strange!

A

The **a** in French sounds like the *a* in "ball" or "wand." Try to pronounce the following words.

1. **ma** 2. **ta** 3. **sa** 4. **chat** 5. **plat** 6. **gratte** 7. **âme** 8. **à**

How did you do? Especially with numbers 4 and 5—did you say too much? Now, listen to the audio file (0PW_04/Tr. 4: Pronunciation, Part B) to see if you got them right.

Did you notice those symbols on top of the last two letters (**â** and **à**)? Those symbols are called *accents*. *An **accent** is a symbol attached to a letter that shows us how to pronounce it and/or helps us know which word we are using.* Sometimes accents change the pronunciation of the letter (don't worry about **a**'s—the pronunciation doesn't change much). Other times, we can tell which of two words we are using by noticing the accent (or the absence of the accent). And like the definition says, sometimes it's both! For example:

- **à** means "to," as in "He's going *to* Morocco."
- **a** means "has," as in "He *has* a plane ticket."[1]
- **paume** [POM] means "palm," as in "It is sitting in the *palm* of your hand."
- **paumé** [POM-AY] means "lost, in the middle of nowhere."[2]
- a **pécheur** is a "sinner" and a **pêcheur** is a "fisherman!"[3]

E

The French **e** is a bit more complicated than the French **a**. It makes several different sounds. Listen to the following words with **e**'s in them (0PW_05/Tr. 5: Pronunciation, Part C):

1. **le** 2. **que** 3. **mets** 4. **ses** 5. **les** 6. **belle** 7. **bête** 8. **changé** 9. **école**
10. **mangé** 11. **mère** 12. **frère**

---
1. In this case, there is a difference in meaning, but no difference in pronunciation.
2. In this case, there is a difference in meaning and in pronunciation.
3. In this case, there is a difference in meaning and in pronunciation.

Listen again to numbers 1–12 (0PW_05/Tr. 5: Pronunciation, Part C), pause the audio file, and then try to *say* the following words:

13. **me**   14. **des**   15. **fête**   16. **sel**   17. **monté**   18. **écart**   19. **père**

Did you get them? Listen to the rest of the audio file to find out (0PW_05/Tr. 5: Pronunciation, Part C).

Let's talk about accents again: Did you notice any change to the way an **e** sounded when it had some kind of accent on it? For example, was the **e** in example 1 the same **e** as in example 18? Definitely not! What did this accent (´) do to the **e**? It made it sound like a very short AY sound, right? We call this accent **aigu** (French for "sharp"). How about the difference between examples 13 and 19? The latter sounds more like an *eh*. We call the accent on the word in example 19 an accent **grave** (Do you remember how to pronounce **grave** from the paragraph on the letter **a**?).

Now, did you notice the funny hat on the **e** in examples 7 and 15? That accent is called a **circonflexe** (sear-con-flex). As you may have heard when listening to the audio file (0PW_05/Tr. 5: Pronunciation, Part C), an **e** with a **circonflexe** has a very similar sound to an **e** with a **grave** (an EH sound). Why do we have to bother with such silly things as accents, then? Aha! Remember that accents already show us how to pronounce a word or show us with *which* word we're dealing. But there is another great reward for knowing one's accents—especially the **circonflexe**! It just so happens that the **circonflexe** accent often clues us into the fact that, a long time ago, there used to be an **s** after the vowel.

So, for example, look at the words **bête** and **fête** again. Imagine these words with an **s** just after the vowel with the **circonflexe** accent: *beste* and *feste*. Hmm, they sound pretty close to some English words you might know, don't they? How about "beast" and "fest" or "festival"? Well, that's just about what they mean in French (**bête** means "beast" and **fête** means "party" or "holiday"). Do you think you're ready to "reconstruct" a few words with the **circonflexe** accent?

The next time your French-speaking friends say that they need to eat their **pâtes** in **hâte** before they go to the **côte** to catch a boat to the **île**, you'll know they just mean that they: need to eat their _____◊ in _____◊◊ before they go to the _____◊◊◊ to catch a boat to the _____◊◊◊◊!

◊pasta ◊◊haste ◊◊◊coast ◊◊◊◊isle (or island)

PRONUNCIATION WIZARD

I

In French, the **i** only makes one sound: EEEE as in "wheel" or "peel." So, it should be pretty easy to guess how the following words sound. Just in case you have any questions, they are also on the audio file (0PW_06/Tr. 6: Pronunciation, Part D).

1. **fil** 2. **pile** 3. **mille** 4. **Gilles** 5. **pif** 6. **cri** 7. **rit** 8. **mine** 9. **midi** 10. **ride**

Attention! In English, if you have the word "bit," and then add the letter *e*, what happens? The word "bite" is formed, and "bite" has a different vowel sound from "bit," right? The same thing is true with the English words "rid" and "ride"—the *e* changes the way you pronounce the *i*.

Now listen closely to the audio file (0PW_06/Tr. 6: Pronunciation, Part D) to see if the French letter **i** changes its sound when there is an **e** in the word. Does it? You'll find the answer in the footnotes.[4]

O

O, good! French **o**'s almost sound like English *o*'s in general. So, **solde** in French sounds pretty close to "sold" in English (except that **les soldes** means "sale" in French!). There are exceptions, however—and these can be tough, so listen attentively to the audio file (0PW_07/Tr. 7: Pronunciation, Part E):

1. **or** 2. **téléphone** 3. **trône** 4. **molle** 5. **folle** 6. **rôle** 7. **bon** 8. **mont** 9. **allons**

H**o**ld the ph**o**ne! What happened to examples 7, 8, and 9? First of all, we *do not pronounce* the final letters. Maybe you can guess why if you remember the rule we learned earlier (when we were talking about **i**'s and **e**'s): That is, only with an **e** at the end of a word can you hear the last few letters. In other words: *If there is no e at the end of the word, there is no guarantee that we will pronounce the last few consonants!*

Second of all, the **o** in examples 7–9 sounds strange, doesn't it? Listen to the pronunciation again. How can you make that sound? Let's try what we call the "hold your nose!" method: First, gently pinch your nose between your thumb and your index finger (as if some stinky French cheese were right next to you). Now, while you hold your nose like that, say the letter **o** like this: "OOOOHHHHHH." As you are holding your fingers to your nose, try to feel if there is any vi-

---

4. The **e** doesn't change the pronunciation at all. In fact, the **e** only makes us pronounce the letter that is before it, so in examples 3 and 4, you pronounce the **l**, in example 8, you pronounce the **n**, and in example 10, you pronounce the **d**. "What?" you say, "That's crazy! Wouldn't you just say those letters anyway?" Well, not always—the word **nid** (nest), for example, is pronounced NEE!

bration in your fingers. If there is *no* vibration, you are making the English *o* sound (as in examples 1–6 in this section). If you can make your fingers (and your nose) vibrate, you are making the French **o** sound of examples 7–9. If you are having trouble, try to imagine the air coming out of not only your mouth, but also your nose as you hold your fingers to it. If you let some air pass through your nose, you will get the right vibrations!

What is the point of all of this? In French, there are some **o** sounds (and **a, i, e,** and **u** sounds!) that are made with the help of your nose. **Any vowel requiring you to let some air pass through your nose is called a *nasal vowel*.** How will you know when you need to use a nasal vowel? It's easy—just look for an **n**!

Listen to the following words from the audio file (0PW_08/Tr. 8: Pronunciation, Part F), and try to repeat them.

1. u**n**   2. br**un**   3. g**an**t   4. ch**an**t   5. **son**t   6. **don**t   7. **men**t   8. **en**   9. fi**n**

U

The French **u** has many different possible pronunciations. It is perhaps the most difficult vowel for English speakers to learn, so be careful. Here is the biggest trap:

The difference between **tout** (all) and **tu** (you).

Whenever you see an **o** before the **u**, you can relax—those two letters combine to form a familiar English *u* sound—oooh—as in the word "you." While they are not *exactly* the same (and you might be able to hear a slight difference on the audio file), the vowels are very similar nonetheless.

In French there are plenty of words that contain this **ou** vowel sound:

1. **tout**   2. **flou**   3. **doux**   4. **goutte**   5. **coûte**

If you'd like to hear these words pronounced, check out the audio file (0PW_09/Tr. 9: Pronunciation, Part G).

Now take a look at these words: **tu, pur, zut, lu, dur, chute, rude, vue.**

How are they different from examples 1–5? There's no **o**. Oh, OK, but no big deal, right? Actually, *yes*, it is a big deal! We need to make a different sound entirely. Let's call it the French *u*. To say the French *u*, here is the trick:

1. Pucker your lips (make them round as though you're about to put on lipstick—guys, you'll just have to pretend you know what you're doing here).
2. Now, hold that position, and try to make the sound EEEE.

What *should* happen is that the EEEE comes out sounding like a weird EW. Voila! The French **u**. Listen to how it sounds with the following words, which you've seen before (0PW_10/Tr. 10: Pronunciation, Part H):

1. **tu**   2. **pur**   3. **zut**   4. **lu**   5. **dur**   6. **chute**   7. **rude**   8. **vue**

Most important, though, the following are pairs of words in which each word has the exact same sounds, except one has the French **u** and the other doesn't. Try to pronounce them yourself before you listen to the audio file (0PW_11/Tr. 11: Pronunciation, Part I).

1a. **tu** (you)   1b. **tout** (all)   2a. **pur** (pure)   2b. **pour** (for)   3a. **lu** (read [past tense])   3b. **loue** (is renting)   4a. **bu** (drank)   4b. **boue** (mud)   5a. **su** (knew)   5b. **sous** (under)

Another reason that **u** in French can be so tough is that it combines with other vowels to make still different sounds from the ones we've learned so far. Listen, for example, to what happens when a **u** meets an **e** inside a word (0PW_12/Tr. 12: Pronunciation, Part J):

1. **deux**   2. **cheveux**   3. **bleu**   4. **feu**   5. **fleur**   6. **beurre**   7. **leur**   8. **peur**

In examples 1–4, the **eu** makes a strange kind of UUHH sound, like you might make if you got hit by a football right in the stomach! In examples 5–8, it's a different kind of sound, this time always with **eur**—it's just a little bit longer than the **eu** of examples 1–4—closer to the *u* in "fur" or "blur."

Y

The letter **y** is easy in French—it's always pronounced like the French **i**—EEEE!

Combinations of Vowels

Often vowels can be right next to each other in a word. We've already seen some examples of this: **o** + **u** = OOOOH and **e** + **u** = UH! (the hit-in-the-stomach sound). There are many other kinds of "mixes," though! These include (0PW_13/Tr. 13: Pronunciation, Part K):

o + **i** = WAH
Examples: **roi** (RWAH), **choix** (CHWAH), **foi** (FWAH)

u + i = WEE
Examples: **puis** (PWEE), **tuile** (TWEEL), **huile** (WEEL)

a + i before **l** = EYE
Examples: **paille** (PIE), **bail** (BUY), **taille** (TIE)

a + i before any other letter = EH
Examples: **trait** (TREH), **faire** (FER), **raide** (RED)

a + u *or* **e + a + u** = OH
Examples: **au** (OH), **taux** (TOH), **beau** (BOH), **eau** (OH)

i + e = EE
Examples: **crie** (CREE), **trie** (TREE), **sortie** (SORTEE)

Consonants

Whew! We're finished with the vowels (for now!). Let's move on to the other letters in the French alphabet, which are called *consonants*. A **consonant** *is a letter that makes you either stop or slow down the air coming up from your lungs, and then out of your mouth.* You'll recognize them in English as:

B C D F G H J K L M N P Q R S T V W X Z

Luckily, they are the same in French! There are a couple of differences between English consonants and French consonants, however—sometimes major differences, and sometimes minor. Let's begin with the major differences between French and English consonants.

Major Differences

R

The French **r** is by fa**r** the toughest letter for English speakers to master. Why, you ask? Well, take a look at the following example sentence with **r** words in it and then listen to the sentence, trying to hear what's different (0PW_14/Tr. 14: Pronunciation, Part L):

Robert[1] a renversé[2] la ratatouille[3] pendant le repas[4].
Robert spilled the ratatouille during the meal.

Le roi[5] René[6] est enrhumé[7]!
King René has a cold!

What did you notice about the pronunciation of the **r**'s in words 1–7? One thing you should definitely have heard is that *to make the French r, the back of your tongue needs to jump up and vibrate against the back your mouth*. Have you ever had a sore throat? What do you do for it (along with taking medicine)? Ever try to gargle salt water? You know, you put some salt in warm water, take a swig, lean your head back, and blow air through the water slowly? Well, the French **r** makes that exact same sound! Only, don't lean your head back when you're speaking French, or people might think you're a little bizarre.

J

In French, the letter **j** is softer than the English *j*. In fact, it is the same SHUH sound as you hear in the words "measure," "bei*g*e," and "pleasure." Listen to the audio file (0PW_15/Tr. 15: Pronunciation, Part M) to hear the following sentences:

Je[1] connais Jacques[2] et son jumeau[3]!
I know James and his twin brother!

Jean[4] ne joue[5] jamais[6] à ce jeu[7]!
John never plays this game!

G

The **g** sound in French changes, just as it does in English. In English, when we say the words "gentle" and "get," the *g* does not make the same sound in each word, right? The first word—gentle—has a *soft g* sound, while the second word—get—has a *hard g* sound. In French, the soft **g** is actually the exact same sound as the French **j** (which makes a SHUH sound)! When do you use the soft **g** in French? Simple: If the letter **g** comes before an **e**, **i**, or **y**. Any other time, the French **g** sounds just like the English hard *g* (*Go get g*reen *g*rapes!). It will be easier to remember this rule when you actually see and hear the words (check out 0PW_16/Tr. 16: Pronunciation, Part N).

Soft G's

George[1] a giflé[2] la girafe[3] géante[4].
George slapped the giant giraffe.

Hard G's

Les gorilles[5] guident[6] les garçons[7] dans les gorges[8].[5]
The gorillas guide the boys through the caves.

Now, a challenge for you! Listen to the following sentence (0PW_17/Tr. 17: Pronunciation, Part O). Then, below each word with a **g**, circle *H* for "hard g" or *S* for "soft g" based on the pronunciation of the word that you hear. The sentence means: "I keep my cheetah in the garage; he's nice, but it bothers people to hear him roar."

Je garde[1] mon guepard[2] dans le garage[3]; il est gentil[4], mais ça gêne[5] les gens[6]
   Ⓗ/ S   Ⓗ/ S   Ⓗ/ S H /Ⓢ   H /Ⓢ   H /Ⓢ   H /Ⓢ
de l'entendre rugir[7].
                 H /Ⓢ

H

The last major difference in consonant sounds between English and French has to do with the tricky little letter **h**. For the most part, the letter **h** makes *absolutely*, *positively* no sound whatsoever. But surely it must make *some* sound, you say? No! Perhaps just a little HU? No! Maybe just a tiny little breath? No, no, no! So then, try your hand at these words:

1. **honnête**   2. **hôpital**   3. **horizon**   4. **homme**

Easy, huh? Just pronounce them "**onnête**," "**ôpital**," "**orizon**," and "**omme**"! (You can also check them out on the audio file 0PW_18/Tr. 18: Pronunciation, Part P.) But 'old your 'orses a minute. You should know one more thing about **h**'s. What happens in English when a *t* or a *c* joins up with an *h* to make *th* or *ch*? You get two new sounds, right? The words "than" and "chop" sound different from the words "tan" and "cop," right? Well, in French, when a **t** joins an **h**, *nothing happens*. But, when a **c** joins up with the letter **h**, we get the sound SSHHH. That means that **thé** (tea—the drink) is pronounced TAY[6] and **thon** (tuna fish) is pronounced TOH![7] On the other hand, **chou** (cabbage) is pronounced SHOO and **choix** (choice) is pronounced SHWA. Try your hand at the following sentences before you listen to them (0PW_19/Tr. 19: Pronunciation, Part Q).

Je suis heureux[1] dans mon hôtel[2], mais j'ai hâte[3] de retourner chez[4] moi.
I'm happy in my hotel, but I'm looking forward to returning home.

---

5. Note that in word 8—**gorges**—there is a hard **g** at the beginning and a soft **g** at the end.
6. Careful, the word **thé** contains an accent **aigu**! (See the accent section in this pronunciation wizard to find out what that means.)
7. And remember, **thon** has a *nasal* vowel—there's an **n** at the end.

Elle cherchait[5] Thomas[6] dans le théâtre[7], mais il chassait[8] des chevaux[9] dehors[10].
She looked for Thomas in the theater, but he was out chasing horses.

Minor Differences

L or LL?

In French you will see words that have two **l**'s in a row: **ville, travailler, grille, paille**, etc. Now, in some of these words, the **ll** makes a normal **l** sound (like "village" in English—the two *l*'s just sound like one, right?). However, in other French words, the **ll** makes the sound of a **y**. There is no easy way to figure out which word is which, but you will get the hang of it as you read and listen to more and more French. Here's a sentence in which all the **ll** words make a **y** sound (0PW_20/Tr. 20: Pronunciation, Part R):

La fille[1] se réveille[2] pour travailler[3].
The girl wakes up to work.

And here's a sentence where all of the **ll** words make an **l** sound (0PW_21/Tr. 21: Pronunciation, Part S):

Elle[4] est la plus belle[5] de la ville[7].
She's the prettiest one in the city.

Q

How do you pronounce the letter **q** in French? That's a quick question to answer: Pronounce it like it's a **k**! Easy, right? So, **roque** is pronounced ROKE and **quatre** is pronounced KAT-RUH. Have a quick listen to the following sentence to really get the feel for French **q**'s (0PW_22/Tr. 22: Pronunciation, Part T):

Quand[1] Quentin[2] a quitté[3] sa classe à quatre[4] heures, il n'avait plus de questions[5].
When Quentin left his class at four o'clock, he didn't have any more questions.

X

Normally, French **x**'s follow the same rules that English *x*'s do. However, there is a special kind of French **x** that can be a trap if you're not careful! Those are the **x**'s at the ends of words (remember the rule "Don't say too much!"). So, check out the following words:

1. **cheveux**   2. **vieux**   3. **courageux**   4. **travaux**   5. **faux**

When you see an **x** at the end of a word like this, just think one thing: "An **x** at the end is *not your friend*!" That means that you don't pronounce it. To hear words 1–5 pronounced, check out the audio file (0PW_23/Tr. 23: Pronunciation, Part U).

Accents (à, é, ô, ç, and others)

We talked about accents before, back in the paragraphs on French **a**'s and **e**'s, but now would be a good time to review the basic guidelines for using accents. So here it is, in full, French's awesome accent action!

Definition: An accent is a symbol attached to a letter that shows us how to pronounce it and/or helps us know which word we are using.

There are four types of accents in French:

- **grave:** `
- **aigu:** ´
- **circonflexe:** ˆ
- **cédille:** ç

Here's how these accents affect different letters:

à	does not change the pronunciation of the **a**; only helps us see which word we are using
â	does not change the pronunciation of the **a**; only helps us see which word we are using
é	changes the pronunciation to a *sharp* AY sound: 1. **écouté** 2. **roulé** 3. **étendre**
è	changes the pronunciation to a relaxed EH sound: 4. **père** 5. **problème** 6. **thème**
ê	same sound as **è**; helps us see which word we are using

î	does not change the pronunciation of the letter; only helps us see which word we are using
ô	does not change the pronunciation of the letter; only helps us see which word we are using
ç	this accent is called the **cédille** and it always makes a **c** sound like an **s**: 7. **français** 8. **façon** 9. **reçu**

To hear words 1–9, listen to audio file 0PW_24/Tr. 24 (Pronunciation, Part V).

Félicitations! (Congratulations!) You've made it to the end of the Pronunciation Wizard. Do make a point to turn back to this section if ever you have a hesitation about how to pronounce a certain letter or word. Of course, the best reference will be your very own ears as you listen to each week's chant, dialogue, and vocabulary on the audio files. One more thing to keep in mind: This pronunciation guide has helped you with the individual sounds of French, which should get you started on your way to pronouncing individual words. But, of course, that's not all there is to master when we think of "speaking with a French accent" or "speaking like a native"—there is also the rhythm of French, and the way words shift their pronunciations depending on what other words surround them, or where the words fall in a sentence. You've got a great opportunity to absorb these other "pronunciation rules" (if you want to call them that—"patterns" might be a better term) as you listen to the dialogues read each week, and hear spoken French on the video. These are patterns that truly are best learned through imitation (with some rare exceptions) rather than listing them all out in some monstrously big and boring appendix. But you will only learn them if you're listening for them! So, remember to pay attention to the rhythms and tones of French as well as the actual pronunciation of French words as you use the audio materials.

MEMORY : GRAMMAR : WORKSHEET : QUIZ

in all of the worksheets and quizzes. So I won't. If a word has multiple translations, I'll indicate this in the *vocabulary list*. As for the worksheet and quiz exercises, unless there is a clear reason (from context) to pick one translation or the other, just choose one and go with it. *The most important thing for you to keep in mind as you learn the vocabulary words in this book is that you are able to imagine a situation in which your choice fits naturally.* So, if you choose, for example, to translate the sentence **Je regarde la carte** as "I look at the map," that's fine, but it is important that you can imagine an appropriate situation in which you would be using that particular meaning (maybe in response to the question "What do you do when you get lost?"). Alternatively, if you translate it as "I am looking at the map," that's also fine—maybe you could imagine someone having asked you, "What are you doing?"

This principle of knowing that different situations might call for different translations for the same word or expression is so key to learning a foreign language that I wanted to bring it to your attention right away here in chapter 1. You'll see quickly just how common the principle is: The vocabulary in chapter 2 will offer another great opportunity to be flexible with your translations!

There is one last thing to point out in this **chapitre**. If you look closely at our second vocabulary word—**j'étudie**—you'll notice that the letter **e** from the word **je** has been squeezed out. Instead of ***je étudie**, we say **j'étudie**. There is an apostrophe (') in the place of the **e** in **je**. This happens very frequently in French when two *vowels* from different words end up next to each other in a sentence—especially the vowel **e**. I'll be sure to point out other examples of this "squeezing" as they come up throughout the book.

TEACHER'S NOTE

Students should *not* be required to supply all possible translations for each exercise: They should only provide one. All of the possible answers will be included in the Answer Key, so don't worry that you'll have to memorize all of the translations just so you can properly grade your students' work. It would be instructive, however, to question students from time to time about the particular choice they've made in translating, such as, "Can you imagine a particular situation that goes along with that translation?" or "In what situation could you imagine using a *different* translation from the one you've provided?"

CHAPITRE 1

Translation

Translate the following words, or groups of words, into English.

1. **la vache**   the cow
2. **la souris**   the mouse
3. **la vache et la souris**   the cow and the mouse
4. **Ça va?**   Answers will vary, but should be one of the following: How are you? How are things going? How is it going? Is everything OK?
5. **la vache avec la carte**   the cow with the map
6. **Je parle.**   I speak/am speaking.
7. **Je parle à la vache.**   I speak/am speaking to the cow.
8. **Je parle français.**   I speak/am speaking French.
9. **Je regarde la souris.**   I look at/am looking at the mouse.
10. **J'étudie la carte avec la vache.**   I study/am studying the map with the cow.

MEMORY : GRAMMAR : WORKSHEET : QUIZ

GRAMMAR

Fill in or circle the correct answer.

1. A *verb* is a word that describes an _____action_____. It tells us what someone is _____doing_____.

2. Circle the three verbs:

   a. town   b. bookshelf   (c. jump)   d. painter   (e. paint)   (f. sleep)

3. In French, **je regarde** means "I look" and never "I am looking."

   Circle one: True   (False)

4. What happens when you have the words **je** + **étudie** (I + study) together in a sentence?

   You get _____j'étudie_____. Why? It is because there are two _____vowels_____ from different words sitting next to each other.

PRONUNCIATION PRACTICE

Go to the Pronunciation Wizard at the beginning of the book and read the part labeled "Introduction." Do the exercises in that section, stopping just before the section labeled "Vowels."

CHAPITRE 1 — 31

New Vocabulary

Fill in the blank with the correct translation for each word.

1.	**je regarde**	I look (at)	6. **la carte**	the map
2.	**j'étudie**	I study	7. **le français**	French
3.	**je parle**	I speak	8. **et**	and
4.	**la vache**	the cow	9. **avec**	with
5.	**la souris**	the mouse	10. **à**	to, at

Translation

Translate the following French sentences into English. (Hint: Remember, depending on the situation, you could translate French verbs such as **je parle** in two different ways in English. In the sentences below, the situation is fairly clear as to which translation would be best, so go ahead and select the most natural one—either *I speak* or *I am speaking*; *I look* or *I am looking*, etc.)

1. No, I don't want to come home right now! **Je parle avec la vache!**
   I am speaking with the cow!

2. None of the other kids talk with the mouse. Only I do. **Je parle avec la souris.**
   I speak with the mouse.

3. "What are you looking at?"
   "**Je regarde la carte.**" I am looking at the map.

4. "Hey, why don't you want to play outside!?"
   "Because! **J'étudie!**" I am studying.

5. My parents want to go on vacation to France, but they're worried because they can't speak any French. I told them to relax, though. **Je parle français!**
   I speak French!

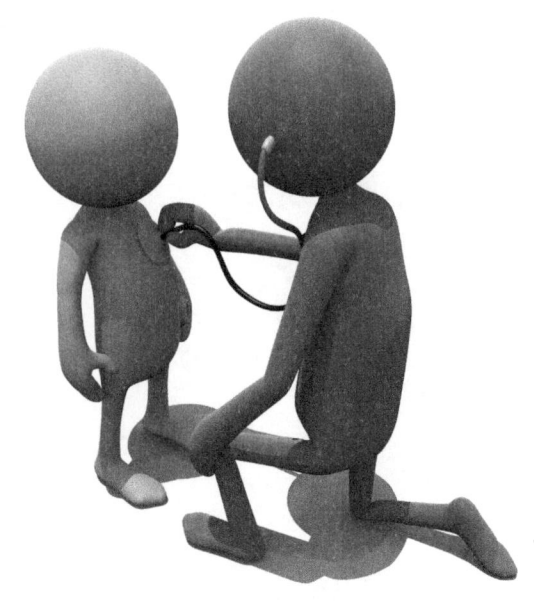

MEMORY : GRAMMAR : WORKSHEET : QUIZ

Dictée!

Listen to the audio file [01_05/Tr. 29] of the **dictée** for this **chapitre**. On the lines provided, write down the three sentences you hear. You do not need to write translations for them, though it's good practice to think through what the English translation would be. You may stop and repeat the audio file several times as you're writing down the sentences.

1. **La vache parle.**   Translation: The cow speaks/is speaking.

2. **La souris étudie.**   Translation: The mouse studies/is studying.

3. **J'étudie et je parle.**   Translation: I study/am studying and I speak/am speaking.

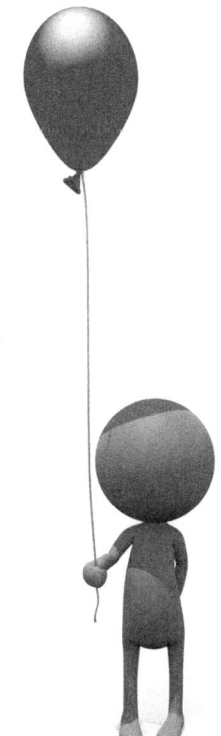

PARTIE I

MEMORY : GRAMMAR : WORKSHEET : QUIZ

CHANT

Fill in the rest of the verb forms of **parler**.

Person	Singular	Plural
1st Person	je parle	nous parlons
2nd Person	tu parles	vous parlez
3rd Person	il/elle parle	ils/elles parlent

TRANSLATION

> **TEACHER'S NOTE**
> As noted in **chapitre** 1, multiple translations will be supplied in the answer key, but students are not required to give all possible translations—just one will suffice.

Translate the following sentences into English.

1. **Il aime la vache.** He likes/loves the cow.
2. **Vous parlez français.** You (all) speak/are speaking French.
3. **Elle travaille pour l'école.** She works/is working for the school.
4. **Nous étudions la carte.** We study/are studying the map.
5. **Nous parlons à la vache.** We talk/speak/are talking/speaking to the cow.
6. **Tu travailles à l'école.** You work/are working at the school.
7. **Elle aime l'école.** She likes/loves the school/school.
8. **Nous aimons la forêt.** We like/love the forest.
9. **Ils regardent la souris.** They look at/are looking at the mouse.
10. **Vous travaillez beaucoup.** You (all) work/are working a lot.

DISSECTION

In this section, you will learn to "dissect" a verb into its different ingredients. For now, you only need to pick *person* and *number*. Following the example we've given you in the first row of the chart, dissect the verbs that follow, and give their translations.

42 PARTIE I

MEMORY : GRAMMAR : WORKSHEET : QUIZ

	Person	Number	Translation
Nous travaillons	first	plural	we work
1. J'étudie	first	singular	I study/am studying
2. Vous aimez	second	plural	you [all] like/love
3. Elle travaille	third	singular	she works/is working
4. Elles travaillent	third	plural	they work/are working
5. Nous marchons	first	plural	we walk/are walking

Grammar

Fill in or circle the correct answer.

1. How many different "ingredients" does a verb form have? __three__

2. Can you name them? __person, number, and tense__

3. Circle two of the questions we should ask when trying to identify a verb form:

    a. What is the name of the person doing the action?

    (b.) How many people are doing the action?

    c. How many times does the person do the action?

    (d.) Who is doing the action?

    e. Is the person doing the action really a certified doctor?

4. English verbs change forms more than French verbs. Circle one: True   (False)

Pronunciation Practice

Go to the Pronunciation Wizard at the beginning of the book and read the part labeled "Vowels." Do the exercises in this section, stopping just before the section labeled "Consonants."

CHAPITRE 2 — 43

MEMORY : GRAMMAR : WORKSHEET : QUIZ

New Vocabulary

Fill in the blank with the correct translation for each word.

1. **aimer, j'aime**	to like/love, I like/love	6. **beaucoup**	a lot, many, very much
2. **marcher, je marche**	to walk, I walk	7. **la forêt**	the forest
3. **travailler, je travaille**	to work, I work	8. **les devoirs**	the homework
4. **la maison**	the house, the home	9. **pour**	for
5. **l'école**	the school	10. **de**	of, from

Review Vocabulary

Fill in the blank with the correct translation for each word.

1. **regarder, je regarde**	to look (at), I look (at)	5. **la souris**	the mouse
2. **et**	and	6. **la vache**	the cow
3. **avec**	with	7. **le français**	French
4. **à**	to, at		

Translation

Translate the following sentences into English.

1. **Elle étudie à l'école.**   She studies/is studying at the school.

2. **Vous aimez les devoirs.**   You (all) like/love homework.

3. **J'étudie à la maison.**   I study at the house/at home. ⚜

4. **Nous parlons français.**   We speak French.

5. **Tu étudies le français.**   You are studying French. ⚜

MEMORY : GRAMMAR : WORKSHEET : QUIZ

Verb Forms

Complete the chart below with the different forms of the verb **travailler** (to work).

Person	Singular	Plural
1st Person	je travaille _____ (I work)	nous travaillons _____ (we work)
2nd Person	tu travailles _____ (you work)	vous travaillez _____ (you [all] work)
3rd Person	il/elle travaille _____ (he/she works)	ils/elles travaillent _____ (they work)

Dictée!

Listen to the audio file [02_05/Tr. 34] of the **dictée** for this **chapitre**. On the lines provided, write down the three sentences you hear. You do not need to write translations for them, though it's good practice to think through what the English translation would be. You may stop and repeat the audio file several times as you're writing down the sentences.

1. **Vous parlez.**   Translation: You [all] speak/are speaking.

2. **Elle travaille beaucoup.**   Translation: She works/is working a lot.

3. **Nous marchons à la maison.**   Translation: We walk/are walking to the house.

> ⚜ TEACHER'S NOTE
>
> Translation #3, from p. 44: The first answer is the literal, word-for-word translation of the French sentence. However, you may notice that it sounds somewhat unnatural in English, if what is meant is that I study at the house that is *my house*. In that case, we'd probably just say, "I study at home." That is a fine translation in this case—maybe even better than the "official" answer. In these types of situations, where a slightly different translation might better capture the meaning than a word-for-word translation does, we will indicate this alongside the word-for-word answers.

> ⚜ TEACHER'S NOTE
>
> Translation #5, from p. 44: In this case, the word **le**, which normally translates as "the," is not translated into English. Occasionally, as you will see, such words simply do not have to be translated, though the reasons for this differ from case to case. We will be sure to let you know whenever this occurs.

CHAPITRE 2 — 45

MEMORY : GRAMMAR : WORKSHEET : QUIZ

CHANT

Complete the chart below with the different conjugations of the verb **finir** (to finish).

Person	Singular	Plural
1st Person	**je finis** _____ (I finish)	**nous finissons** (we finish)
2nd Person	**tu finis** _____ (you finish)	**vous finissez** _____ (you [all] finish)
3rd Person	**il/elle finit** (he/she finishes)	**ils/elles finissent** _____ (they finish)

TRANSLATION

1. **Elles mangent beaucoup.** They eat/are eating a lot.

2. **Tu finis les devoirs.** You finish/are finishing the homework.

3. **Tu aimes manger!** You love/like to eat!

4. **Je cherche le chat.** I look for/am looking for the cat.

5. **Vous cherchez le chien.** You (all) look for/are looking for the dog.

6. **Nous cherchons le chien avec la voiture.** We look for/are looking for the dog with the car.

MEMORY : GRAMMAR : WORKSHEET : QUIZ

7. Elle reste à la maison. She stays/is staying at the house.

8. Elle finit les devoirs. She finishes/is finishing the homework.

9. Nous réussissons à l'école. We succeed/are succeeding at school.

10. Vous finissez les devoirs. You (all) finish/are finishing the homework.

Dissection

Following the example we've given you, dissect the verbs that follow, and give their translations.

	Person	Number	Translation
Vous finissez	second	plural	you all finish
Nous finissons	first	plural	we finish
Je réussis	first	singular	I succeed
Ils réussissent	third	plural	they succeed
Vous réussissez	second	plural	you (all) succeed
Ils restent	third	plural	they stay

MEMORY : GRAMMAR : WORKSHEET : QUIZ

Grammar

Circle or fill in the correct answer.

1. Circle the letter of the correct name of the *different forms* of a verb that change depending on who (*person*) and how many (*number*) are doing the action?

    a. computation

    b. constellation

    ⓒ. conjugation

    d. combination

    e. constipation

2. The form of a verb that has no changed endings—the "original" form of a verb—is called the __infinitive__.

3. If you listed the verb **parler** (to speak/talk) in all of the different forms (I speak, you speak, he speaks, etc.) and then next to it you listed the verb **chercher** (to look for) in all of the different forms, you would find the exact same pattern if you *erased* the _____ of the word. Circle the correct answer.

    ⓐ. beginning

    b. end

    c. last letter

    d. first letter

Pronunciation Practice

Go to the Pronunciation Wizard at the beginning of the book and read the part labeled "Consonants." Do the exercises in that section, stopping just before the section labeled "Accents."

Mission Infinity

Below is a large group of verbs. You've seen some of the verbs before—others you have not. Don't worry about translating anything; your mission is to pick out all of the infinitives *just by the forms*, and write them in the list on the side. Can you find all eleven?

mange	arrête	fournir	remplissent	
chanter	cuisinons	fabriquons	attachez	
vieillir	promets	rigoler	chassent	
déménagez	créez	trient	plient	
travaillons	écouter	dorment	lave	
parle	frémissons	discutez	pardonnent	
téléphonent	grignote	montons	grimpez	
ranges	retirons	cultivez	élèvent	
ajoutez	mélanges	trichent	manquez	
regardent	développez	imaginent	tomber	
vole	glisses	tournent	gagnent	
pleurer	crient	finis	choisissez	
marchons	gémir	naviguent	sortez	
allumes	tape	dansez	jouer	
remplir	communique	mènent	rougissent	
cherchons	trouve	appeler	aimons	

Infinitives:

1. fournir
2. chanter
3. tomber
4. vieillir
5. rigoler
6. pleurer
7. écouter
8. gémir
9. jouer
10. remplir
11. appeler

CHAPITRE 3 — 55

New Vocabulary

Fill in the blank with the correct translation for each word.

1. **finir, je finis**	to finish, I finish	6. **manger, je mange**	to eat, I eat
2. **réussir, je réussis**	to succeed, I succeed	7. **le chien**	the dog
3. **espérer [que], j'espère [que]**	to hope [that], I hope [that]	8. **le chat**	the cat
4. **chercher, je cherche**	to look (for), I look (for)	9. **la voiture**	the car
5. **rester, je reste**	to stay, I stay	10. **ou**	or

Review Vocabulary

Fill in the blank with the correct translation for each word.

1. **aimer, j'aime**	to like/love, I like/love	6. **avec**	with
2. **marcher**	to walk	7. **la maison**	the house, the home
3. **parler, je parle**	to speak, I speak	8. **la forêt**	the forest
4. **beaucoup**	a lot, many, very much	9. **étudier, j'étudie**	to study, I study
5. **la carte**	the map	10. **de**	of, from

Translation

Translate the following sentences into English.

1. **Tu aimes étudier à la maison.** You like/love to study at the house/at home.

MEMORY : GRAMMAR : WORKSHEET : QUIZ

2. **Elle réussit à l'école.** She succeeds/is succeeding at school.

3. **J'aime finir les devoirs!** I like/love to finish homework!

4. **Nous espérons parler français.** We hope to speak French.

5. **J'espère que tu réussis.** I hope that you succeed. ⚜

6. **Ils restent avec la voiture.** They stay/are staying with the car.

Conjugation Chart

Complete the following chart with the different conjugations of the verb **réussir** (to succeed).

Person	Singular	Plural
1st Person	**je réussis** (I succeed)	nous réussissons _____ (we succeed)
2nd Person	tu réussis _____ (you succeed)	vous réussissez _____ (you [all] succeed)
3rd Person	il/elle réussit _____ (he/she succeeds)	ils/elles réussissent _____ (they succeed)

Teacher's Note

⚜ Technically, "to hope" here could be construed as progressive—"I am hoping that you succeed"—but it is an unusual form and it's unlikely that students will translate this sentence that way.

CHAPITRE 3

MEMORY : GRAMMAR : WORKSHEET : QUIZ

Dictée!

Listen to the audio file [03_05/Tr. 39] of the **dictée** for this **chapitre**. On the lines provided, write down the three sentences you hear. You do not need to write translations for them, though it's good practice to think through what the English translation would be. You may stop and repeat the audio file several times as you're writing down the sentences.

1. **Il finit les devoirs.**   Translation: He finishes/is finishing the homework.

2. **Ils finissent les devoirs.**   Translation: They finish/are finishing the homework.

3. **Tu restes dans la voiture.**   Translation: You stay/are staying in the car.

✚ REMARQUE

In this dictée you will hear the word **dans**, which sounds a little like "dah" (but with a nasally vowel). **Dans** means "in."

MEMORY : GRAMMAR : WORKSHEET : QUIZ

CHANT

Complete the chart below based on this **chapitre**'s chant. The third-person plural form has been filled in for you.

Person	Singular	Plural
1st person	I (_____je_____)	we (_____nous_____)
2nd person	you (_____tu_____)	you (all) (_____vous_____)
3rd person	he/she (_____il/elle_____)	they (**ils/elles**)

TU OR VOUS

Your family and your friends seem to be getting into trouble lately. You need to ask them if they are OK. How would you ask them in French? Following the examples we've given you, decide whether you'd say **tu** (you) or **vous** (you), and then circle the correct answer.

Examples:

Your brothers fell out of their canoe. You ask them, "Are _____ OK?" (tu /**(vous)**) ["Brothers" is *plural*.]

Your mom has had the hiccups for five hours. You ask her, "Are _____ OK?" (**(tu)**/ vous) [Mom is singular.]

1. Your best friend was just stung by a jellyfish. You ask him, "Are _____ OK?"

   (**(tu)**/ vous)

2. Your cousins all got sick from eating junk food. You ask them, "Are _____ OK?"

   (tu /**(vous)**)

3. Your parents fell into the pool at a fancy dinner party. You ask them, "Are _____ OK?" (tu /**(vous)**)

4. Your friend just ate a really spicy pepper and is now turning purple. You ask her, "Are _____ OK?" (**(tu)**/ vous)

5. Your teammates look like they're about to pass out. You ask them, "Are _____ OK?" (tu /(vous))

Picking the Right Pronoun

In this exercise you need to figure out which subject pronoun from the following list is the best one to replace the underlined subject in the sentence. Then, rewrite the sentence with the *subject pronoun* (SP) that fits best. Finally, translate (T) the new sentence. Follow the examples:

Subject Pronouns: je   tu   il   elle   nous   vous   ils   elles

Examples:

a. <u>Jean</u> marche avec Aurélie.

   SP: **Il marche avec Aurélie.**

   T: He is walking with Aurélie.

b. <u>My brothers and I</u> étudions à l'école.

   SP: **Nous étudions à l'école.**

   T: We study at the school.

1. <u>Aurélie</u> marche dans la forêt.

   SP: Elle marche dans la forêt.

   T: She walks/is walking in the forest.

2. <u>Jean</u> mange avec Aurélie.

   SP: Il mange avec Aurélie.

   T: He eats/is eating with Aurélie.

3. <u>The boy scouts</u> marchent dans la forêt.

   SP: Ils marchent dans la forêt.

   T: They walk/are walking in the forest.

4. <u>You and your friends</u> mangez beaucoup.

   SP: Vous mangez beaucoup.

   T: You eat/are eating a lot.

MEMORY : GRAMMAR : WORKSHEET : QUIZ

5. <u>The girls</u> **regardent le chien dans le zoo.**

    SP: Elles regardent le chien dans le zoo.

    T: They look at/are looking at the dog in the zoo.

6. <u>My friends and I</u> **aimons chanter.**

    SP: Nous aimons chanter.

    T: We like/love to sing.

7. <u>Le chien</u> **habite avec le chat.**

    SP: Il habite avec le chat.

    T: He lives/is living with the cat.

Translation

1. **La vache marche avec la souris.** The cow walks/is walking with the mouse.

2. **Ils marchent vers l'école.** They walk/are walking toward the school.

3. **Tu regardes la vache et la souris.** You look at/are looking at the cow and the mouse.

4. **Nous regardons le chat dans l'école.** We look at/are looking at the cat in the school.

5. **Chut! Je pense que le chat étudie.** Shh! I think that the cat is studying.

6. **Le chien étudie avec le chat.** The dog studies/is studying with the cat.

7. **Le chien et le chat étudient.** The dog and the cat study/are studying.

8. **Je pense qu'ils habitent à l'école.** _I think that they live/are living at the school._

> ✚ **REMARQUE**
> Huh? What's happening with sentence 8? **Je pense** *qu'ils* **habitent**? What happened to the **e** from **que**? Well, as in some other cases we've seen, the **e** gets booted out when **que** meets up against a word beginning with a vowel. And, as usual, an apostrophe is there to tie the two words together.

Grammar

Circle or fill in the correct answer.

1. The words **je**, **tu**, **il/elle**, **nous**, **vous**, **ils/elles** form a group called ___subject___ ___pronouns___.

2. What is special about the group of words mentioned in question 1? They can ___replace___ *any* subject in a sentence, such as "Steve," "you and Tom," "birthday cake," or "my friends."

3. If you wanted to use a subject pronoun instead of "the acrobat" in the sentence "The acrobat always needs a hand," which of the following words would you choose?

   a. we   b. you   (c. she)   d. I   e. they

4. In French, there are two forms of the word "you." They are ___tu___ and ___vous___. We use ___vous___ when there are two or more people who are part of the "you," and we use ___tu___ when the "you" is only one person.

Pronunciation Practice

This is your last pronunciation practice! Go to the Pronunciation Wizard at the beginning of the book and read the part labeled "Accents." When you are listening to the audio file, be sure to listen carefully for the different sounds letters make when they have accents on them!

MEMORY : GRAMMAR : WORKSHEET : QUIZ

Confused Conjugation

The verb charts below have gone haywire! Try to fix them by crossing out the incorrect forms of the verb, like this: **~~parlez~~**. Then, write the correct forms of the verb in the correct blanks. We've done one chart for you. **Note:** Some of the forms may be correct, so don't cross those out!

Example: **Parler** (to speak)

Person	Singular	Plural
1st Person	je ~~parlent~~ _parle_ (I speak)	nous ~~parle~~ _parlons_ (we speak)
2nd Person	tu ~~parlez~~ _parles_ (you speak)	vous ~~parle~~ _parlez_ (you [all] speak)
3rd Person	il/elle parle _____ (he/she speaks)	ils/elles parlent _____ (they speak)

1. **Manger** (to eat):

Person	Singular	Plural
1st Person	je ~~mangez~~ _mange_ (I eat)	nous ~~mangez~~ _mangeons_ (we eat)
2nd Person	tu manges _____ (you eat)	vous mangez _____ (you [all] eat)
3rd Person	il/elle ~~mangeons~~ _mange_ (he/she eats)	ils/elles ~~mange~~ _mangent_ (they eat)

2. **Réussir** (to succeed):

Person	Singular	Plural
1st Person	je réussis _____ (I succeed)	nous ~~réussit~~ _réussissons_ (we succeed)
2nd Person	tu ~~réussissez~~ _réussis_ (you succeed)	vous ~~réussis~~ _réussissez_ (you [all] succeed)
3rd Person	il/elle ~~réussissons~~ _réussit_ (he/she succeeds)	ils/elles réussissent _____ (they succeed)

CHAPITRE 4

New Vocabulary

Fill in the blank with the correct translation for each word.

1. **trouver, je trouve**	to find, I find	6. **le zoo**	the zoo
2. **chanter, je chante**	to sing, I sing	7. **l'arbre**	the tree
3. **penser (que), je pense (que)**	to think [that], I think [that]	8. **dans**	in
4. **préférer, je préfère**	to prefer, I prefer	9. **ici**	here
5. **habiter, j'habite**	to live, I live	10. **vers**	toward

Review Vocabulary

Fill in the blank with the correct translation for each word.

1. **chercher, je cherche**	to look (for), I look (for)	6. **pour**	for
2. **rester, je reste**	to stay, I stay	7. **travailler, je travaille**	to work, I work
3. **finir, je finis**	to finish, I finish	8. **désolé** ⚜	sorry
4. **chat**	cat	9. **l'école**	the school
5. **la voiture**	the car	10. **les devoirs**	the homework

Teacher's Note

This word, **désolé**, is actually taken from a Conversation Journal, rather than from one of the vocabulary lists, so if students are confused you can point that out to them. Note that future review vocabulary items may also be drawn from the Conversation Journals.

MEMORY : GRAMMAR : WORKSHEET : QUIZ

CHANT

Fill in the English translations of the French words in the following chart. The third-person plural has been filled in for you.

Person	Singular	Plural
1st Person	je (_____I_____)	nous (_____we_____)
2nd Person	tu (_____you_____)	vous (_____you_____)
3rd Person	il/elle (_____he/she_____)	ils/elles (they)

TRANSLATION

Translate the following sentences into English.

1. **La vache et la souris préfèrent marcher dans la forêt.** _The cow and the mouse prefer to walk in the forest._

2. **Je mange avec la vache. Nous mangeons.** _I eat/am eating with the cow. We eat/are eating._

3. **Nous préférons manger dans la maison.** _We prefer to eat in the house._

4. **La vache préfère rester dans la voiture.** _The cow prefers to stay in the car._

5. **Le chat marche vers la forêt.** _The cat walks/is walking toward the forest._

CHAPITRE 4

MEMORY : GRAMMAR : WORKSHEET : QUIZ

Dictée!

Listen to the audio file [04_05/Tr. 44] of the **dictée** for this **chapitre**. On the lines provided, write down the three sentences you hear. You do not need to write translations for them, though it's good practice to think through what the English translation would be. You may stop and repeat the audio file several times as you're writing down the sentences.

1. **Vous chantez beaucoup.**   Translation: You sing/are singing a lot.

2. **Nous habitons dans la maison.**   Translation: We live/are living in the house.

3. **Jean et Aurélie habitent dans le zoo.**   Translation: Jean and Aurélie live/are living in the zoo.

Review

CHAPITRE 5 CINQ

Now that you have learned forty French words (actually, more if you count the Conversation Journals!), it is time to review them and make sure you won't forget them! Remember to practice reciting these words for five to ten minutes every day. Even better, sing or chant them.

Try to supply the English meaning for each French word in the list below. For each word that you miss, put a check in the box next to that word. Then work really hard on those "checked words" until you have them mastered. If you want to, write any words that stump you on a separate piece of paper with the English beside them and practice them until you have them memorized. You may even want to make yourself flash cards of the words that you missed and practice them with a friend or your parents. At least once every day this week, review the list of all the words you've learned so far.

	French	English		French	English
☐	regarder, je regarde	to look (at), I look (at)	☐	aimer, j'aime	to like/to love, I like/I love
☐	étudier, j'étudie	to study, I study	☐	marcher, je marche	to walk, I walk
☐	parler, je parle	to speak/talk, I speak/talk	☐	travailler, je travaille	to work, I work
☐	la vache	the cow	☐	la maison	the house, the home
☐	la souris	the mouse	☐	l'école	the school
☐	la carte	the map	☐	beaucoup	a lot
☐	français	French	☐	la forêt	the forest
☐	et	and	☐	les devoirs	homework
☐	avec	with	☐	pour	for
☐	à	to, at	☐	de	of, from

Review

French	English		French	English
☐ finir, je finis	to finish, I finish		☐ trouver, je trouve	to find, I find
☐ réussir, je réussis	to succeed, I succeed		☐ chanter, je chante	to sing, I sing
☐ espérer [que], j'espère [que]	to hope [that], I hope [that]		☐ penser [que], je pense [que]	to think [that], I think [that]
☐ chercher, je cherche	to look (for), I look (for)		☐ préférer, je préfère	to prefer, I prefer
☐ rester, je reste	to stay, I stay		☐ habiter, j'habite	to live, I live
☐ manger, je mange	to eat, I eat		☐ le zoo	the zoo
☐ le chien	the dog		☐ l'arbre	the tree
☐ le chat	the cat		☐ dans	in
☐ la voiture	the car		☐ ici	here
☐ ou	or		☐ vers	toward

Let's Go on a Field Trip!

It's time for a field trip. Let's climb into an imaginary time machine and travel back more than 2,000 years to ancient Rome. Picture the huge, beautiful stone buildings rising above you. Feel the hot stones of the busy city streets beneath your feet and the Mediterranean breezes blowing the edges of your toga as we walk through the marketplace. Listen: All the people bustling around you with baskets of grapes and olives are speaking a language called Latin. In fact, "Mediterranean," the name of the sea nearest Rome, is made up of two Latin words, *medi* and *terra*, meaning "middle" and "earth." Here in the year AD 10, the Roman Empire is the most powerful force in the world, and the Mediterranean Sea is at its center.

REVIEW

Let's put your new understanding of cognates to work. In the following lists of words, draw lines to match the French words on the left with their English cognates on the right.

Professions

1. **artiste**
2. **musicien**
3. **acteur**
4. **biologiste**
5. **plombier**
6. **mécanicien**

a. plumber
b. biologist
c. artist
d. actor
e. mechanic
f. musician

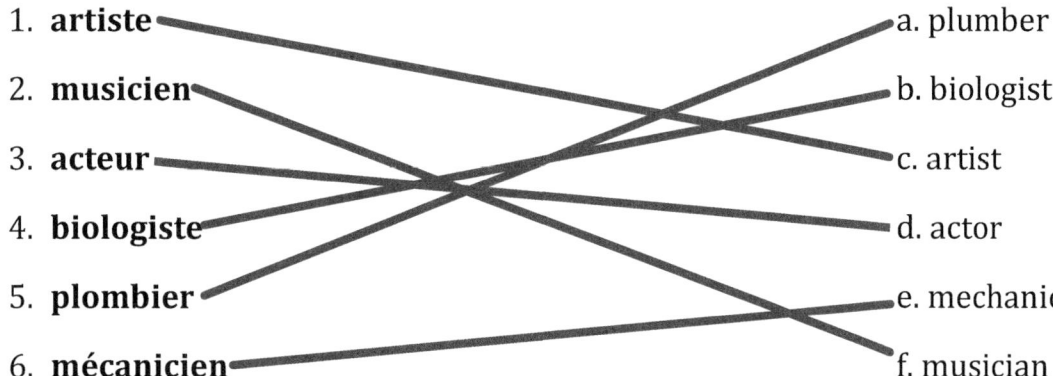

Adjectifs (Adjectives)

1. **rapide**
2. **intéressant**
3. **fameux**
4. **curieux**
5. **difficile**
6. **typique**

a. difficult
b. famous
c. typical
d. rapid
e. interesting
f. curious

Verbes (Verbs)

1. **danser**
2. **créer**
3. **changer**
4. **défendre**
5. **maintenir**
6. **observer**

a. to change
b. to defend
c. to maintain
d. to dance
e. to observe
f. to create

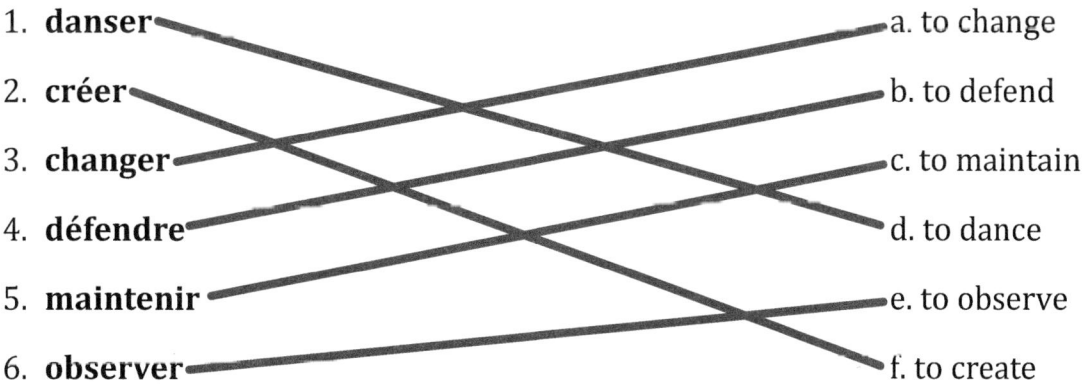

REVIEW

Verbs: Dissecting and Translating

In the following exercise, first identify the person and number of the verb. (This is the same exercise that you did in the Worksheet sections of **chapitres** 2 and 3.) Then, when you have finished, go back and translate each verb into English, as we have done in the example at the top.

French Verb	Person	Number	Translation
Example: ils parl*ent*	third	plural	they speak/talk ⚜
nous étud*ions*	first	plural	we study
je trouv*e*	first	singular	I find
elle mang*e*	third	singular	she eats
ils regard*ent*	third	plural	they look (at)
nous chant*ons*	first	plural	we sing
ils réuss*issent*	third	plural	they succeed
tu fin*is*	second	singular	you finish
nous aim*ons*	first	plural	we like/love
je pens*e*	first	singular	I think

> ✟ **Remarque**
>
> Have you noticed something over the last few chapters about the *first-person singular* form of a verb and the *third-person singular* form? It is often the same! This makes life a little bit easier for us, since we don't have to learn as many different forms of one verb. Be on the lookout for "identical twin" forms throughout the different verb charts in this book.

Say It Aloud!

In this section, we want you to practice *saying aloud* some of the French you've learned. If you need it, you can use the Pronunciation Wizard to help. The following are six very short sentences in English. Your job is to *translate* these sentences into French—either in your head, or on this page, next to the sentence—and then *say them aloud*. Check your answers by listening to the audio file (05_01/Tr. 45).

1. I am looking at the cow. **Je regarde la vache.**

Review

2. You are walking with the mouse. **Tu marches/Vous marchez avec la souris.**

3. We are succeeding. **Nous réussissons.**

4. You, M. Dupont, are singing. **Vous, M. Dupont, chantez.**

5. They are finishing. **Ils/Elles finissent.**

6. She is eating. **Elle mange.**

> **TEACHER'S NOTE**
> From page 80: Also acceptable are translations with the *-ing* form, such as "they are speaking/talking," etc.

Traduction (Translation)

Suivez l'exemple (Follow the example).

Example: **La vache mange devant la ferme. Elle mange devant la ferme.**

Translation: The cow is eating in front of the farm. It is eating in front of the farm.

1. **Le serpent cherche la souris. Il cherche la souris.** The snake looks for/is looking for the mouse. It looks for/is looking for the mouse.

2. **Le renard mange le fromage. Il mange le fromage.** The fox eats/is eating the cheese. It eats/is eating the cheese.

3. **La vache regarde la grange. Elle regarde la grange.** The cow looks at/is looking at the barn. It looks at/is looking at the barn.

4. **La souris chante dans la grange. Elle chante dans la grange.** The mouse sings/is singing in the barn. It sings/is singing in the barn.

5. **Le cochon mange avec le renard. Il mange avec le renard.** The pig eats/is eating with the fox. It eats/is eating with the fox.

6. **La grange est devant la maison. Elle est devant la maison.** (Hint: **est** = is.) The barn is in front of the house/the home. It is in front of the house/the home.

7. **L'école est à côté de la maison. Elle est à côté de la maison.** The school is next to the house/the home. It is next to the house/the home.

8. **La voiture est devant la maison. Elle est devant la maison.** The car is in front of the house/the home. It is in front of the house/the home.

9. **La souris marche vers la ville. Elle marche vers la ville.** The mouse walks/is walking toward the city. It walks/is walking toward the city.

MEMORY : GRAMMAR : WORKSHEET : QUIZ

10. **Le chat joue avec la vache dans la grange. Il joue avec la vache dans la grange.**
    The cat plays/is playing with the cow in the barn. It plays/is playing with the cow in the barn.

Grammaire*

*(We bet you can guess what this means!)

Circle or fill in the correct answer. When more than one answer seems possible, choose the best answer.

1. A *noun* is:

    a. a person

    b. a person or a place

    c. a person or a thing

    (d.) a person, a place, or a thing

    e. expensive

2. If a *noun* has a *masculine gender*, that means that it must be a boy. True or **(False)**

3. If a *noun* has a *feminine gender*, that means that:

    a. it is a girl

    (b.) you might use the word **la** before it

    c. it is something that females generally use

    d. it will only be said by female speakers

    e. if you say it, you will turn into a woman unless you are one already

4. In French, _____ nouns have *gender*.

    (a.) all

    b. some

    c. seventy-four

    d. very few

5. In French, the word "it" is the same word as "he" sometimes and the same word as "she" other times. It changes depending on what the "it" is. **(True)** or False

---

88 — PARTIE 2

MEMORY : GRAMMAR : WORKSHEET : QUIZ

Substitution

Substitute the word **il** or **elle** for the *noun* under each blank in the sentences below. Follow the example.

Example: <u> Il </u> **cherche la maison.** (It is looking for the house.)
(**Le chat**)

1. <u>   Il   </u> **aime la voiture!** (It loves the car!)
   (**Le chien**)

2. <u>   Elle   </u> **marche vers la grange.** (It is walking toward the barn.)
   (**La vache**)

3. <u>   Elle   </u> **est² devant le château.** (It is in front of the castle.)
   (**La voiture**)

4. <u>   Il   </u> **est à côté de la maison.** (It is next to the house.)
   (**Le serpent**)

5. <u>   Il   </u> **trouve la souris dans la grange.** (It finds the mouse in the barn.)
   (**Le cochon**)

---

2. You should remember what **est** means from Worksheet **Traduction** (Translation) exercise 6, but if you don't, go ahead and look back at that exercise to refresh your memory.

MEMORY : GRAMMAR : WORKSHEET : QUIZ

New Vocabulary

Fill in the blank with the correct translation for each word.

1.	jouer, je joue	to play, I play	7. le village	the village
2.	le cochon	the pig	8. la grange	the barn
3.	le renard	the fox	9. la ville	the city
4.	le serpent	the snake	10. à côté de	next to
5.	le fromage	the cheese	11. devant	in front of
6.	la ferme	the farm		

Review Vocabulary

Fill in the blank with the correct translation for each word.

1.	l'arbre	the tree	6. bien sûr	of course
2.	dans	in	7. aimer, j'aime	to like/love, I like/love
3.	ici	here	8. regarder, je regarde	to look (at), I look (at)
4.	espérer [que], j'espère [que]	to hope [that], I hope [that]	9. bonsoir	good evening
5.	réussir, je réussis	to succeed, I succeed	10. alors	so

PARTIE 2

MEMORY : GRAMMAR : WORKSHEET : QUIZ

Traduction

Translate the following sentences into French.

1. Lucie is speaking to M. Dupont. She is speaking to M. Dupont.

    Translation: __Lucie parle à M. Dupont. Elle parle à M. Dupont.__

2. The pig walks to the school. It walks to the school.

    Translation: __Le cochon marche à l'école. Il marche à l'école.__

3. The snake is³ next to the barn. It is next to the barn.

    Translation: __Le serpent est à côté de la grange. Il est à côté de la grange.__

4. The cow is playing with the cat. It is playing with the cat.

    Translation: __La vache joue avec le chat. Elle joue avec le chat.__

5. The cat is eating cheese. It is eating cheese.

    Translation: __Le chat mange le fromage. Il mange le fromage.__

Teacher's Note

From page 90: Recall the difference between the parentheses surrounding the word "at" in the English translation of **regarder** and the square brackets surrounding the word "that" in the translation of **espérer**—the square brackets, we noted in **chapitre** 3, mean that you actually need to translate the French word **que** (if it's used), whereas the regular parentheses in the translation of **regarder** indicate that you *can* supply the word "at" if it would make the translation more natural, even though the equivalent French word is not used. We said before that it is "built in," so to speak, to the verb itself.

3. You've seen the French word for "is" several times now. Do you remember what it is? If not, look back at exercise 6 of the Worksheet **Traduction** section.

MEMORY : GRAMMAR : WORKSHEET : QUIZ

Dictée!

Listen to the audio file [06_05/Tr. 50] of the **dictée** for this **chapitre**. On the lines provided, write down the three sentences you hear. You do not need to write translations for them, though it's good practice to think through what the English translation would be. You may stop and repeat the audio file several times as you're writing down the sentences.

1. **Le cochon mange dans la grange.**   Translation: The pig eats/is eating in the barn.

2. **Nous jouons à côté de la ville.**   Translation: We play/are playing next to the city.

3. **La vache et le serpent jouent dans la ferme.**   Translation: The cow and the snake play/are playing on the farm.

TEACHER'S NOTE
We normally translate the word **dans** as "in," but in the expression **dans la ferme**, it can be translated as "on"—"on the farm."

Le Renard. Of course. **Il habite** due north of here, I believe, **dans les montagnes**. But, come, you should stay and hear more of my tales!

Aurélie. Ah oui! Je préfère rester ici!

Jean. Non, Aurélie. We need to get a move on. And besides, I'm hungry. **Monsieur Renard** [*Jean glares at him*], you are welcome to join us, but we'll be on our way now.

Le Renard. Ah! Alors, non, merci. Je reste ici. Ciao!

Chant [07_02/Tr. 52]

> **Teacher's Note**
> This should be sung/chanted to the tune of "Deck the Halls."

Gender

Deck the halls with masculine nouns . . . **le, le, le, le, le, le, le, le, le**
Don't forget the feminine ones . . . **la, la, la, la, la, la, la, la, la**
Now the plural version hear . . . **les, les, les, les, les, les, les, les, les**
Articles that fill your ear . . . **le, le, le, le, la, la, la, les, les**

Vocabulaire [07_03/Tr. 53]

Français	Anglais
tomber, je tombe	to fall, I fall
voler, je vole	to fly, I fly
l'oiseau	the bird
la fleur	the flower
la montagne	the mountain
le champ	the field
le vent	the wind
sur	on, on top of
derrière	behind
loin (de)	far (from)

MEMORY : GRAMMAR : WORKSHEET : QUIZ

Traduction

Suivez l'exemple (Follow the example).

Exemple:[3] **Les chiens mangent les devoirs. Ils mangent les devoirs.**

Translation: The dogs eat the homework. They eat the homework.

1. **L'oiseau vole dans le vent. Il vole dans le vent.** The bird flies/is flying in the wind. It flies/is flying in the wind.

2. **Les arbres tombent dans le vent. Ils tombent dans le vent.** The trees fall/are falling in the wind. They fall/are falling in the wind.

3. **Les renards marchent dans la forêt. Ils marchent dans la forêt.** The foxes walk/are walking in the forest. They walk/are walking in the forest.

4. **Les vaches marchent dans le champ. Elles marchent dans le champ.** The cows walk/are walking in the field. They walk/are walking in the field.

5. **La vache étudie la carte. Elle étudie la carte.** The cow studies/is studying the map. It studies/is studying the map.

---

[3]. Did you notice that this word looked a little weird? Did you think that we just misspelled "example" or did you guess that **exemple** is the French word for "example"? If you did, you've got a good eye. Keep it up!

CHAPITRE 7

MEMORY : GRAMMAR : WORKSHEET : QUIZ

Say It Aloud!

First translate each sentence, then go back and read the French sentences aloud. You'll hear the French versions read in the audio file (07_05/Tr. 55).

1. **Elle marche à la maison.** _She walks/is walking to the house/the home._

2. **Elles marchent à la maison.** _They walk/are walking to the house/the home._

3. **Il travaille à l'école.** _He works/is working at the school._

4. **Ils travaillent à l'école.** _They work/are working at the school._

5. **L'arbre tombe dans le vent. Il tombe dans le vent.** _The tree falls/is falling in the wind. It falls/is falling in the wind._

Grammaire

Circle the correct answers.

1. The word **ils** (by itself) is pronounced exactly the same as the word **il**.

    (True) or False

2. The word **elles** (by itself) is pronounced exactly the same as the word **elle**.

    (True) or False

3. In French, there is more than one word for "it." You can say:

    (a.) **il** if the noun is masculine and **elle** if the noun is feminine

    b. **ils** if the noun is masculine and **elles** if the noun is feminine

    c. **la** if the noun is masculine and **le** if the noun is feminine

    d. **le** if the noun is masculine and **la** if the noun is feminine

    e. **ooh** if the noun is masculine and **là là** if the noun is feminine

MEMORY : GRAMMAR : WORKSHEET : QUIZ

4. If you are trying to replace the masculine subject **les chiens** with a subject pronoun in the sentence, "They [the dogs] are looking for the cat," the word you would choose for "they" is:

   a. **les**

   b. **il**

   (c.) **ils**

   d. **elles**

   e. **elle**

5. Given a group of animals, some of which are masculine (**les chiens**) and some of which are feminine (**les vaches**), how would you say, "They [the dogs and the cows] are looking for the cat?" The word you would choose for "they" is:

   a. **les**

   b. **il**

   (c.) **ils**

   d. **elles**

   e. **elle**

6. If you see a noun such as **l'école** in French, the fact that you cannot see **le** or **la** in front of the word means that:

   a. It probably has no gender.

   b. It might have gender, but you can't tell what it is.

   c. It definitely has gender, but you will never know what it is.

   (d.) It definitely has gender, but you might need to use other clues to find out what the gender is.

   e. It probably never wanted gender anyway.

New Vocabulary

Fill in the blank with the correct translation for each word.

1.	**tomber, il tombe**	to fall, it falls	6. **le champ**	the field
2.	**voler, il vole**	to fly, it flies	7. **le vent**	the wind
3.	**l'oiseau**	the bird	8. **sur**	on, on top of
4.	**la fleur**	the flower	9. **derrière**	behind
5.	**la montagne**	the mountain	10. **loin (de)**	far (from)

Review Vocabulary

Fill in the blank with the correct translation for each word.

1.	**la ville**	the city	6. **chien**	dog
2.	**à côté de**	next to	7. **étudier, j'étudie**	to study, I study
3.	**le renard**	the fox	8. **trouver, je trouve**	to find, I find
4.	**le cochon**	the pig	9. **chut!**	Shhhh!, Be quiet!
5.	**bientôt**	soon	10. **au revoir**	good-bye

Traduction

Translate the sentences from French to English *or* from English to French.

1. **Jean et Aurélie habitent dans le zoo. Ils habitent dans le zoo.** Jean and Aurélie live/are living in the zoo. They live/are living in the zoo.

MEMORY : GRAMMAR : WORKSHEET : QUIZ

2. **Jean et Aurélie préfèrent rester dans le zoo.** They prefer staying in the zoo. <u>Jean and Aurélie prefer to stay in the zoo. Ils préfèrent rester dans le zoo.</u>

3. Aurélie likes to study maps. She likes to study maps. <u>Aurélie aime étudier les cartes. Elle aime étudier les cartes.</u>

4. **Le serpent aime rester à côté de l'école. Il aime rester à côté de l'école.** <u>The snake likes to stay next to the school. It likes to stay next to the school.</u>

5. Foxes prefer to eat cheese. They prefer to eat cheese. <u>Les renards préfèrent manger le fromage. Ils préfèrent manger le fromage.</u>

Dictée!

Listen to the audio file [07_06/Tr. 56] of the **dictée** for this **chapitre**. On the lines provided, write down the three sentences you hear. You do not need to write translations for them, though it's good practice to think through what the English translation would be. You may stop and repeat the audio file several times as you're writing down the sentences.

1. <u>L'oiseau vole loin de l'arbre.</u>   Translation: The bird flies/is flying far from the tree.

2. <u>Les fleurs tombent dans le vent.</u>   Translation: The flowers fall/are falling in the wind.

3. <u>Nous aimons marcher dans les montagnes.</u>   Translation: We like to walk in the mountains.

TEACHER'S NOTE

From p. 102: Now we know that **il** or **elle**, depending on the context, can be translated as "it," especially when we're talking about a non-human or an inanimate object. You can accept either answer—he/it or she/it—as long as it makes sense and as long as students know *why* they are choosing the translation they choose.

Pop Quiz: Verb Review!

OK, so it's not really a quiz, but with this week's new irregular verb being introduced, you'd better remember what the regular ones look like! Fill in the blanks. We've done a couple of them for you.

1. **Parler** *(to speak)—A Regular* **-er** *Verb*

Person	Singular	Plural
1st Person	**je** parle (I speak)	**nous** parlons (we speak)
2nd Person	**tu** parles (you speak)	**vous** parlez (you speak)
3rd Person	**il/elle** parle (he/she/it speaks)	**ils/elles** parlent (they, m./f. speak)

2. **Avoir** *(to have)—Our New Irregular Verb!*

Person	Singular	Plural
1st Person	j'ai (I have)	nous avons (we have)
2nd Person	**tu as** (you have)	vous avez (you have)
3rd Person	il/elle a (he/she/it has)	**ils/elles** ils/elles ont (they, m./f. have)

Traduction

1. **La fille a sept frères.** The girl has seven brothers.

2. **Les frères ont une sœur.** The brothers have a sister.

MEMORY : GRAMMAR : WORKSHEET : QUIZ

3. **La mère a huit[3] enfants.** _The mother has eight children._

4. **Ils habitent dans une maison.** _They live/are living in a house._

5. **Ils ont des chiens.** _They have dogs._

6. **Nous habitons dans un zoo.** _We live/are living in a zoo._

7. **Nous avons deux sœurs.** _We have two sisters._

8. **Les souris habitent dans la grange.** _The mice live/are living in the barn._

9. **Un serpent habite dans l'arbre.** _A snake lives/is living in the tree._

10. **Le garçon parle avec une fille.** _The boy speaks/talks/is speaking/is talking with a girl._

Substitution

In the following sentences, you have a choice of three articles under each blank. Fill in the blank with the appropriate article. We've provided an example to start you off.

Exemple:

  Un chat cherche la maison. (A cat is looking for the house.)
(un / une / des)

1. **Je travaille dans ___une___ grange.** (I am working in a barn.)
   (un / une / des)

2. **J'ai ___des___ frères.** (I have brothers.)
   (un / une / des)

3. **Hint:** What number **chapitre** are we in?

MEMORY : GRAMMAR : WORKSHEET : QUIZ

3. **Nous regardons** ____**une**____ **montagne.** (We are looking at a mountain.)
   (un / une / des)

4. **Vous avez** ____**un**____ **chat et** ____**un**____ **renard?** (You have a cat and a fox?)
   (un / une / des)   (un / une / des)

5. **Tu as** ____**des**____ **devoirs?** (You have homework?)
   (un / une / des)

Grammaire

Circle the correct answers.

1. The verb **avoir** is called _____ because it doesn't follow the normal pattern of conjugations we've learned.

   (a.) irregular   b. regular   c. strange   d. common

2. In the list below, the only *indefinite article* is (circle one):

   a. **la**   b. **les**   c. **le**   (d.) **un**   e. **uh huh**

3. If you see the word **une** in French, it can be translated:

   a. the   b. a   (c.) a *or* an   d. feminine   e. feminist

4. If someone was looking for his birthday cake (**gâteau**), and you were storing it for him, what would you tell him?

   a. **J'ai un gâteau.**   b. **J'aime le gâteau.**   (c.) **J'ai le gâteau.**

   d. **Tu as un gâteau.**   e. **La vache mange le gâteau.**

5. If you didn't know, could you tell what gender the noun **devoirs** is by looking at the indefinite article **des**, as in **J'ai *des* devoirs**?

   a. Yes, it is clearly masculine.

   b. Yes, it is clearly feminine.

   (c.) No, you need other clues to figure it out (or a French dictionary to help you).

   d. Yes, it is plural, so we ... errr ... hmmmmm ...

   e. Homework? You're giving us more homework?

CHAPITRE 8

Nouveau (New) Vocabulaire

Fill in the blank with the correct translation for each word.

1. **avoir, j'ai** — to have, I have
2. **un, deux, trois, quatre, cinq, six, sept, huit, neuf, dix, onze, douze** — one, two, three, four, five, six, seven, eight, nine, ten, eleven, twelve
3. **une famille** — a family
4. **un père** — a father
5. **une mère** — a mother
6. **un enfant** — a child
7. **un frère** — a brother
8. **une sœur** — a sister
9. **une fille** — a girl
10. **un garçon** — a boy

Ancien (Old) Vocabulaire

Fill in the blank with the correct translation for each word.

1. **le vent** — the wind
2. **la fleur** — the flower
3. **tomber, je tombe** — to fall, I fall
4. **le champ** — the field
5. **devant** — in front of
6. **la ferme** — the farm
7. **manger, je mange** — to eat, I eat
8. **bienvenue** — welcome
9. **chanter, je chante** — to sing, I sing
10. **Allons-y!** — Let's go!

MEMORY : GRAMMAR : WORKSHEET : QUIZ

Chaotic Conjugation

Oh, no! The computer has crashed and all of our verb charts in this **chapitre** have been scrambled! Help us set things straight by putting the correct forms of the verb in the correct boxes. If there is a form in a box that is incorrect, cross it out like this: **avez**. Then write the correct form next to it. If you come across forms that you think are correct, you can leave them alone. Check out the Worksheet in **chapitre** 4 if you need a reminder on how to do this.

1. Avoir *(to have)*

Person	Singular	Plural
1st Person	j'~~avez~~ j'ai (I have)	nous ~~ai~~ avons (we have)
2nd Person	tu ~~ont~~ as (you have)	vous avez (you have)
3rd Person	il/elle ~~avons~~ a (he/she/it has)	ils/elles ~~as~~ ont (they have)

2. Étudier *(to study)*

Person	Singular	Plural
1st Person	~~je étudions~~ j'étudie (I study)	nous ~~étudient~~ étudions (we study)
2nd Person	tu ~~étudie~~ étudies (you study)	vous ~~étudient~~ étudiez (you study)
3rd Person	il/elle ~~étudies~~ étudie (he/she/it studies)	ils/elles étudient _____ (they study)

CHAPITRE 8

Number Ladder

Help put the rungs of this number ladder in the right order. Starting from the bottom with "one," and working your way up to finishing at the top with the number "twelve," write the correct number on each rung.

cinq _____ **douze** _____

douze _____ **onze** _____

neuf _____ **dix** _____

un _____ **neuf** _____

deux _____ **huit** _____

onze _____ **sept** _____

huit _____ **six** _____

sept _____ **cinq** _____

trois _____ **quatre** _____

dix _____ **trois** _____

six _____ **deux** _____

quatre _____ **un** _____

MEMORY : GRAMMAR : WORKSHEET : QUIZ

Traduction

Translate the following sentences into English.

1. **Une famille habite dans une ferme.**[4]   A family lives/is living on a farm.

2. **Le père et la mère ont cinq enfants.**   The father and the mother have five children.

3. **Les deux frères aiment beaucoup les trois sœurs.**   The two brothers like/love the three sisters a lot/very much.

4. **Ils travaillent dans la ferme avec des chats et des chiens.**   They work/are working on the farm with cats and dogs.

5. **Les chiens jouent avec les chats, et les chats jouent avec les souris!**   The dogs play with the cats, and the cats play with the mice!

6. **La famille a aussi des cochons et une vache.**   The family also has pigs and a cow.

7. **La vache marche dans un champ.**   The cow walks/is walking in a field.

8. **Elle mange beaucoup.**   It eats/is eating a lot.

---

4. **Désolé** (sorry), this one is a little tricky. In this case, the expression **dans une ferme** should be translated as "on a farm," as opposed to "in a farm." This is another very interesting example of something that happens all the time when translating between languages: Word-for-word translation does not always work. That is because different languages describe the world differently. Think about it: Is there anything more logical about saying "on a farm" than "in a farm"? If an apple is on a table, then the table is under the apple, right? So, if you live "on a farm" does that mean the farm is under you? Not really! It's all around you, of course, so even the English expression "on a farm" is not 100 percent literal. In any case, the point is that sometimes you'll notice that a French expression describes a situation in a different way than it is described in English, so you cannot simply translate word for word back into English: You have to capture the idea being expressed in a way that sounds natural to "English ears." Here's one more neat example of this: In English we say that someone is "in a photo," and in French we say that someone is "on a photo" (**sur une photo**). Think about how each language's way of describing this might make sense.

MEMORY : GRAMMAR : WORKSHEET : QUIZ

9. Elle mange dans la grange, et dans le champ. <u>It eats/is eating in the barn, and in the</u>
   <u>field.</u>

10. Elle aime manger dans la maison aussi! <u>It likes/loves to eat in the house, too!</u>

FIN (The End)

Dictée!

Listen to the audio file [08_05/Tr. 61] of the **dictée** for this **chapitre**. On the lines provided, write down the three sentences you hear. You do not need to write translations for them, though it's good practice to think through what the English translation would be. You may stop and repeat the audio file several times as you're writing down the sentences.

1. **J'ai deux frères.**   Translation: I have two brothers.

2. **La fille a trois sœurs.**   Translation: The girl has three sisters.

3. **Nous avons une famille avec beaucoup de garçons.**   Translation: We have a family with a lot of boys.

TEACHER'S NOTE

From page 115: We've translated **elle** as "it" because we are assuming this pronoun refers to **la vache** (i.e., a non-human), from the preceding sentences. However, if students translate the word as "she," thinking it is separate from the preceding sentences, that is fine. Even if they translate it as "she" thinking of the cow as a female cow, in the way that people may talk about their pets as "he" or "she," this would be fine as well.

MEMORY : GRAMMAR : WORKSHEET : QUIZ

Traduction

Translate the following sentences into English.

1. **J'ai des amis.** I have friends.
2. **J'ai faim.** I am hungry.
3. **Nous avons des chevaux.** We have horses.
4. **Nous avons faim!** We are hungry!
5. **Nous avons faim parce que nous travaillons.** We are hungry because we are working.
6. **Tu as combien de frères?** You have how many brothers?
7. **Tu as sept frères?** You have seven brothers?
8. **Ils ont faim?** They are hungry?
9. **Vous avez combien d'animaux?** You have how many animals?
10. **Vous avez faim?** You're hungry? (Are you hungry?)

La petite fille a combien de . . . ? (The little girl from our story has lots of different things.)

Imagine that Jean and Aurélie are getting ready for bed at night after meeting the little girl. They're asking each other questions about her family and the animals they own. Look at the pictures below and follow the directions.

1. Write a **combien** question for each picture.
2. Say how many of each thing she has. Follow the example of **frères** (brothers) below.

Exemple: 1. Elle a combien de frères?   2. Elle a sept frères.

CHAPITRE 9 — 121

MEMORY : GRAMMAR : WORKSHEET : QUIZ

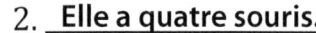

1. **Elle a combien de souris?**   2. **Elle a quatre souris.**

1. **Elle a combien de cochons?**   2. **Elle a cinq cochons.**

1. **Elle a combien de animaux?**   2. **Elle a trois animaux.**

Grammaire

Circle the correct answers.

1. If you pronounced the words **jeu** and **jeux** in French, would you hear a difference?

    a. Yes, but there is not a very big difference.

    (b.) No, there is no difference at all.

    c. Yes, whenever you add letters to a word in French, you change the sound.

    d. Yes, it would be just like the difference between "so" and "sox" in English!

2. In French, if a word is *plural*, it might end with:

    a. **-uz**, **-aus**, or **-xs**   b. **-i**, **-ae**, or **-ox**   c. **-ai**, **-ss**, or **-euz**   (d.) **-s**, **-eux**, or **-aux**

3. In French, to say, "You are hungry," we actually use the expression:

    a. You hunger.   b. You're full of hunger.   (c.) You have hunger.
    d. You are hungered.   e. You have hungry.

PARTIE 2

Nouveau Vocabulaire

Fill in the blank with the correct translation for each word.

1. **avoir faim, j'ai faim**	to be hungry, I am hungry	6. **un jeu**	a game
2. **un ami**	a friend	7. **un problème**	a problem
3. **un animal**	an animal	8. **mais**	but
4. **un cadeau**	a present, a gift	9. **si**	if
5. **un cheval**	a horse	10. **toujours**	always

Ancien Vocabulaire

Fill in the blank with the correct translation for each word.

1. **une sœur**	a sister	6. **aussi**	too, also
2. **un enfant**	a child	7. **avoir, j'ai**	to have, I have
		8. **la montagne**	the mountain
3. **une famille**	a family		
4. **sur**	on, on top of	9. **réussir, je réussis**	to succeed, I succeed
5. **voler, je vole**	to fly, I fly	10. **espérer [que], j'espère [que]**	to hope [that], I hope [that]

MEMORY : GRAMMAR : WORKSHEET : QUIZ

Traduction

1. Les chiens marchent dans la forêt. Ils cherchent des animaux! <u>The dogs walk/are walking in the forest. They look for/are looking for animals!</u>

2. Les frères et le père ont faim. Ils ont faim. <u>The brothers and the father are hungry. They are hungry.</u>

3. Les oiseaux volent beaucoup. Ils chantent dans les arbres. <u>The birds fly a lot. They sing in the trees.</u>

4. La grange a beaucoup d'animaux! Elle a quatre chevaux et cinq cochons. <u>The barn has many animals! It has four horses and five pigs.</u>

5. Aurélie espère jouer avec les animaux. Elle aime les jeux. <u>Aurélie hopes to play with the animals. She likes/loves games.</u>

"Pluringular"~Plural or Singular?

In each of the exercises below, you will see a word. If the word is singular, you need to make it plural. If it is plural, you need to make it singular. If you want a bonus point, write down the meaning of the *newly changed word*. Check out the example below and then try it for yourself.

Original	Plural or Singular?	Bonus Point!
cochons	cochon	pig
1. vache	vaches	cows
2. sœur	sœurs	sisters
3. animal	animaux	animals
4. arbres	arbre	tree
5. jeux	jeu	game
6. château	châteaux	castles[2]

2. You haven't seen this word before, but I bet you can guess what the plural form—castles—is in French!

MEMORY : GRAMMAR : WORKSHEET : QUIZ

Original	Plural or Singular?	Bonus Point!
7. **cadeaux**	cadeau	present, gift
8. **elle**[3]	elles	they (f.)
9. **cheval**	chevaux	horses
10. **maisons**	maison	house
11. **voitures**	voiture	car
12. **ils**	il	he
13. **ami**	amis	friends

Dictée!

Listen to the audio file [09_07/Tr. 68] of the **dictée** for this **chapitre**. On the lines provided, write down the three sentences you hear. You do not need to write translations for them, though it's good practice to think through what the English translation would be. You may stop and repeat the audio file several times as you're writing down the sentences.

1. **Vous avez faim?** Translation: You're hungry? or Are you hungry?

2. **Ils ont des vaches et des chevaux.** Translation: They have cows and horses.

3. **Les animaux ont toujours faim.** Translation: The animals are always hungry.

---

3. For the meaning of this word, see if you can write down not just the English translation, but also to what gender (masculine or feminine) it refers.

CHAPITRE 10

REVIEW

Another four **chapitres** have come and gone! Let's first take time to review the new vocabulary that you've learned. Just as in the last review **chapitre**, place a check mark next to any words you cannot remember and make sure to work extra hard on those problem words before starting the next **chapitre**.

French	English
☐ jouer, je joue	to play, I play
☐ le cochon	the pig
☐ le renard	the fox
☐ le serpent	the snake
☐ le fromage	the cheese
☐ la ferme	the farm
☐ le village	the village
☐ la grange	the barn
☐ la ville	the city
☐ à côté de	next to
☐ devant	in front of
☐ tomber, je tombe	to fall, I fall
☐ voler, il vole	to fly, I fly
☐ l'oiseau	the bird

French	English
☐ la fleur	the flower
☐ la montagne	the mountain
☐ le champ	the field
☐ le vent	the wind
☐ sur	on, on top of
☐ derrière	behind
☐ loin (de)	far (from)
☐ avoir, j'ai	to have, I have
☐ un, deux, trois, quatre, cinq, six, sept, huit, neuf, dix, onze, douze	one, two, three, four, five, six, seven, eight, nine, ten, eleven, twelve
☐ une famille	a family
☐ un père	a father

REVIEW

French	English
☐ une mère	a mother
☐ un enfant	a child
☐ un frère	a brother
☐ une sœur	a sister
☐ une fille	a girl
☐ un garçon	a boy
☐ avoir faim, j'ai faim	to be hungry, I am hungry
☐ un ami	a friend

French	English
☐ un animal	an animal
☐ un cadeau	a present, a gift
☐ un cheval	a horse
☐ un jeu	a game
☐ un problème	a problem
☐ mais	but
☐ si	if
☐ toujours	always

My List of Words to Master

So that you can easily review the words you are having difficulty remembering, write them down on the lines provided below.

1. _____
2. _____
3. _____
4. _____
5. _____
6. _____
7. _____
8. _____
9. _____
10. _____

11. _____
12. _____
13. _____
14. _____
15. _____
16. _____
17. _____
18. _____
19. _____
20. _____

CHAPITRE 10

REVIEW

Verbs (Chapitres 1–3)

Fill in or circle the correct answers.

1. Define *verb*. **A verb is a word that expresses an action. It tells us what someone or something is *doing*.**

2. Circle four verbs in the group of words below:

arbre	une	maison	à côté de	(avons)	chat
sur	fille	cinq	montagne	serpents	des
l'école	(étudiez)	(regardent)	terre	vache	ours
de	dix	(manges)			

3. Define *conjugation*. **A conjugation is the pattern that a verb follows when changing forms to agree with different subjects.**

4. The *infinitive* of a verb is the form which has no ____**changed**____ ending. (That is, it is not conjugated.)

5. Circle the verb that is an *infinitive*.

   a. **trouver** ⟵ circled

   b. **volez**

   c. **habitons**

   d. **avez**

   e. **avons**

6. If a verb is in the *singular form*, how many people are doing the action of the verb? ____**one**____

7. Put an *S* next to the following verbs that are singular and a *P* next to verbs that are plural. The first two verbs are in English to give you a head start! (Hint: Some of the verbs could be singular *or* plural, so for those write *S/P*.)

   __S__ I speak.

   __P__ They speak.

   __P__ Nous avons.

CHAPITRE 10 — 129

REVIEW

__S__ Tu cherches.

__S__ Elle mange.

__S/P__ Vous jouez.

8. If you pronounced all of the following verb forms out loud, which ones would sound exactly the same? Circle them:

(parle)   parlons   (parles)   parlez   (parlent)

Nouns and Pronouns (Chapitres 4, 6, 7, 9)

Fill in or circle the correct answer.

1. A noun is a ____person____, a ____place____, or a ____thing____.

2. A noun that *does the action* in a sentence is called a ____subject____.

3. *Gender* tells you whether a noun is ____masculine____ or ____feminine____.

4. What is special about *subject pronouns*? They can ____replace____ any subject in a sentence.

5. Use a subject pronoun to transform this sentence: **Le garçon parle français.** __Il__ **parle français.**

6. ((Tu)/ Vous) is the singular form of "you," whereas (tu /(vous)) is the plural form. This is basically the difference between "you" and "you guys" or "((you all)/ those people)."

   However, sometimes (tu /(vous)) is used not as a plural pronoun, but rather as the formal or polite form of "you" for a person to whom you want to show ((respect)/ happiness).

   We don't have this distinction in English, but French does separate between a familiar, "comfortable" form of "you," which is ((tu)/ vous), and a formal, respect-showing form of "you," which is (tu /(vous)).

REVIEW

7. How would you make the singular word **château** (castle) plural in French?

    a. **châteaus**

    b. **châteas**

    c. **chêetahs**

    ⓓ **châteaux**

    e. **châts**

8. Is there a difference in pronunciation between the singular word **vache** and the plural form **vaches**?

    a. There is a small difference.

    b. There is a huge difference.

    ⓒ There is no difference at all.

    d. It depends if the word is masculine or feminine.

9. If you see a noun such as **l'école** in French, the fact that you do not see **le** or **la** in front of the word means that:

    a. It probably has no gender.

    b. It might have gender, but you can't tell what it is.

    c. It definitely has gender, but you will never know what it is.

    ⓓ It definitely has gender, but you might need to use other clues to find out what the gender is.

    e. It probably never wanted gender anyway.

REVIEW

Articles (Chapitres 8–9)

Fill in or circle the correct answer.

1. Circle the three English articles in the following list of words:

   (a)   there   (an)   these   (the)   that

   Now write those three words in the spaces below. Draw a line from those three *English* articles to the corresponding *French* articles below them, which could possibly mean the same thing (you should have more than three lines!):

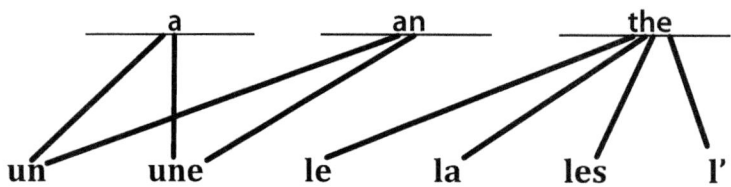

2. Which of the French articles above are *definite articles*? __le, la, les, l'__

3. Which of the French articles above are *indefinite articles*? __un, une__

Conjugation

Do you remember all of the different verb forms you've learned so far? Well, now is the time to use them! Complete the following chart using the forms you've learned for the regular **-er** and **-ir** verbs (see **chapitre** 3) and the irregular verb **avoir** (see **chapitre** 8). We've done a few of them for you.

Person	Parler	Finir	Avoir	Habiter
1st Person Singular	je parle	je finis	j'ai	j'habite
2nd Person Singular	tu parles	tu finis	tu as	tu habites
3rd Person Singular (m.)	il parle	il finit	il a	il habite
1st Person Plural	nous parlons	nous finissons	nous avons	nous habitons
2nd Person Plural	vous parlez	vous finissez	vous avez	vous habitez
3rd Person Plural (f.)	elles parlent	elles finissent	elles ont	elles habitent

We should also add another combination that you might run into: **de** plus the definite article **l'**. Remember that article we use when the noun begins with a vowel? (*a* school = **une école**, but *the* school = **l'école**). Here's what happens when **de** meets **l'** ... nothing!

l'   de + l' → de l'   **Nous travaillons près *de* l'école.** (We work near the school.)

The Curious Haves, Part 2

You might have noticed in this **chapitre**'s vocabulary that we have another unexpected phrase that uses the verb **avoir** (to have). This time, we learn that to say, "I am afraid of" something in French, we again use **avoir**: **J'ai** (I *have*) **peur de** (fear of) something. Here is another chart to remind you how **avoir** works when used in this new expression.

Person	Singular	Plural
1st Person	**j'ai peur de** (I am afraid of)	**nous avons peur de** (we are afraid of)
2nd Person	**tu as peur de** (you are afraid of)	**vous avez peur de** (you are afraid of)
3rd Person	**il/elle a peur de** (he/she/it is afraid of)	**ils/elles ont peur de** (they are afraid of)

Notice also that this verb, **avoir peur de**, uses the daring **de**. That means you'll have to remember the rules we've learned when it comes time to say *what*, exactly, you're afraid of—**d'un serpent? du vent? des chevaux?**

TEACHER'S NOTE

Translations: **d'un serpent?** (of a snake?) **du vent?** (of the wind?) **des chevaux?** (of horses?).

MEMORY : GRAMMAR : WORKSHEET : QUIZ

Traduction

1. **Aurélie et Jean marchent près du fleuve.** Aurélie and Jean walk/are walking near the river.

2. **Aurélie a peur du fleuve.** Aurélie is afraid of the river.

3. **Jean a aussi peur de l'eau.**[1] Jean is also afraid of the water.

4. **Les poissons nagent dans l'eau.** The fish swim/are swimming in the water.

5. **Le cousin de Monsieur l'Oiseau habite près du lac.** The cousin of Monsieur l'Oiseau lives/is living near the lake.

Find a Partner for the Daring De!

Below you'll see several different words, or groups of words, all beginning with the daring **de**. Next to those words are words of different number (singular or plural) and gender (masculine and feminine). Use your knowledge of gender and number and circle the word that goes with the form of the daring **de**. The first one is done for you.

d'une	(montagne)	jeux	du	(vent)	gâteaux
de l'	voiture	(arbre)	des	(écoles)	arbre
d'une	arbre	(maison)	de l'	amis	(ami)
d'un	(cheval)	chevaux	d'une	cousin	(famille)
des	(amis)	jeu	du	(lac)	lacs
de la	animal	(vache)			

1. Sometimes, the order of words in French is a bit different from how it would be in English. That is the case here, so try to think of the overall meaning before you translate (i.e., don't just go word for word), and see if you can figure out a natural English translation. You'll learn more about word order later on in this book.

Grammaire

1. The sentence, **Le chat habite dans *la maison de la famille*,** can mean either:

    a. The cat lives in *the house of the family*. **OR** The cat lives *with the family*.

    b. The cat lives in *the house of the family*. **OR** The cat's family lives in *the house*.

    (c.) The cat lives in *the house of the family*. **OR** The cat lives in *the family's house*.

    d. The cat house-sits *for the family*. **OR** The cat needs to be put *in a home*.

2. What happens when the word **de** lands next to the word **les** in a sentence?

    (a.) They form the word **des**.

    b. They form the word **d'un**.

    c. Nothing happens.

    d. They form the word **d'une**.

    e. They form the word **deles**.

3. What happens when the word **de** lands next to the word **la** in a sentence?

    a. They form the word **dela**.

    b. They form the word **des**.

    (c.) Nothing happens.

    d. They form the word **d'une**.

    e. They form the word **du**.

4. What happens when the word **de** lands next to the word **le** in a sentence?

    a. They form the word **di**.

    b. They form the word **dude**.

    c. Nothing happens.

    d. They form the word **due**.

    (e.) They form the word **du**.

5. In French, to say "You are afraid," we actually use the expression:

    a. You fear.

    (b.) You have fear.

    c. You're fearful.

    d. You are scared.

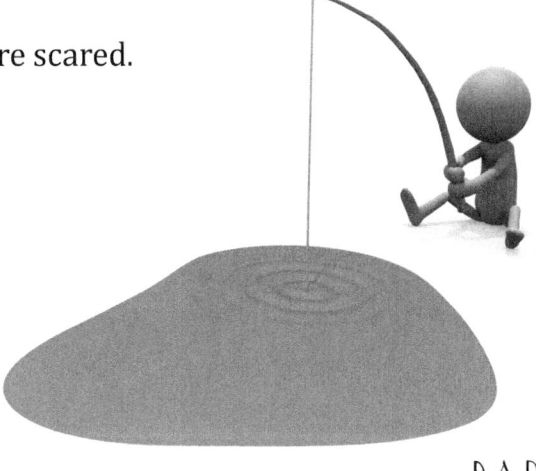

MEMORY : GRAMMAR : WORKSHEET : QUIZ

Nouveau Vocabulaire

Fill in the blank with the correct translation for each word.

1. **avoir peur de, j'ai peur de**	to be afraid of, I'm afraid of	6. **la plage**		the beach
2. **nager, je nage**	to swim, I swim	7. **le poisson**		the fish
3. **la mer**	the sea	8. **l'eau**		the water
4. **le fleuve**	the river	9. **près (de)**		near (to), close (to)
5. **le lac**	the lake	10. **tout**		everything, all

Ancien Vocabulaire

Fill in the blank with the correct translation for each word.

1. **ami**	friend	6. **à**		to, at
2. **ou**	or	7. **ici**		here
3. **de**	of, from	8. **si**		if
4. **sur**	on, on top of	9. **mais**		but
5. **et**	and	10. **dans**		in

MEMORY : GRAMMAR : WORKSHEET : QUIZ

Traduction

Translate the following sentences into English.

1. **Vous avez peur des chiens?** You're afraid of dogs?
2. **Non! Nous avons peur des chats.** No! We're afraid of cats!
3. **Tu as peur des poissons?** You're afraid of fish?
4. **Non! J'ai peur des fleuves.** No! I'm afraid of rivers!
5. **Le frère et la sœur ont peur du serpent?** The brother and the sister are afraid of the snake?
6. **Oui! Ils ont peur du serpent.** Yes! They're afraid of the snake.
7. **Ils ont peur de la plage?** They're afraid of the beach?
8. **Non! Ils ont peur de l'eau!** No! They're afraid of the water!
9. **Ils ont peur des souris?** They're afraid of mice?
10. **Oui! Ils ont peur des souris!** Yes! They're afraid of mice!
11. **Ils ont peur des animaux?** They're afraid of animals?
12. **Non! Ils ont peur de tout!** No! They're afraid of everything!

Dictée!

Listen to the audio file [11_05/Tr. 74] of the **dictée** for this **chapitre**. On the lines provided, write down the three sentences you hear. You do not need to write translations for them, though it's good practice to think through what the English translation would be. You may stop and repeat the audio file several times as you're writing down the sentences.

1. **Nous jouons près du lac.** Translation: We're playing near the lake.
2. **Aurélie a peur des serpents.** Translation: Aurélie is afraid of snakes.
3. **Aurélie et Jean ont peur de l'eau.** Translation: Aurélie and Jean are afraid of water (or "the water").

The Curious Haves, Part 3

Encore! "Encore" means "more," as in "Let's have some more." We figured you liked the curious haves so much that you'd want an encore, so here it is, our third installment. In this **chapitre**, you're learning an extremely useful expression: **avoir besoin de** (to need). Just as **avoir peur de** means, literally, "to have *fear* of" something, this **chapitre**'s expression means "to have *need* of" something. **Besoin**, then, simply means "need." **J'ai besoin d'une sœur** (I need a sister). **Nous avons besoin d'une maison** (We need a house). Also, just like **avoir peur de**, our new expression uses the word **de** again, so you'll have even more opportunities to practice combining words with **de**. And everyone *needs* that. See if you can fill in the following chart with all of the different forms of **avoir** in **avoir besoin de**.

Person	Singular	Plural
1st Person	j'____ai____ besoin de (I need)	nous ____avons____ besoin de (we need)
2nd Person	tu ____as____ besoin de (you need)	vous ____avez____ besoin de (you need)
3rd Person	il/elle ____a____ besoin de (he/she/it needs)	ils/elles ____ont____ besoin de (they need)

MEMORY : GRAMMAR : WORKSHEET : QUIZ

Traduction

Translate the following sentences into English.

1. **L'oiseau habite près d'un lac magnifique.**[3] The bird lives/is living near a magnificent lake.

2. **L'oiseau a besoin de manger.** The bird needs to eat.

3. **L'oiseau cherche des poissons délicieux.** The bird looks for/is looking for delicious fish.

4. **Il aime manger des poissons délicieux, mais il préfère manger du fromage blanc, ou du fromage jaune.** He likes/loves to eat delicious fish, but he prefers to eat white cheese, or yellow cheese.

5. **Jean aime manger tout fromage.** Jean likes/loves to eat all cheese.

6. **Aurélie aime parler avec l'oiseau amusant.** Aurélie likes/loves to talk with the funny bird.

7. **Aurélie et Jean ont besoin de trouver la ville.** Aurélie and Jean need to find the city.

Out of Order

There's been a grammatical tornado again! In each of the exercises below, use the English sentence as a clue to put the mixed-up French sentence back in order and write the correct sentence on the line provided. **Suivez l'exemple** (Follow the example):

Exemple: A purple bird is flying next to the house. à côté de oiseau vole violet un la maison

Un oiseau violet vole à côté de la maison.

[3]. Note: We're talking about **Le Héron** (The Heron) from our story here, of course.

CHAPITRE 12 — 147

MEMORY : GRAMMAR : WORKSHEET : QUIZ

1. An orange fish is swimming in the lake.   **lac dans le nage poisson orange un**

   Un poisson orange nage dans le lac.

2. The girls are eating a delicious cheese.   **fromage mangent les un délicieux filles**

   Les filles mangent un fromage délicieux.

3. The black pig eats everything.   **tout le mange cochon noir**

   Le cochon noir mange tout.

4. A lazy horse is walking on the mountain.   **un montagne la cheval marche paresseux sur**

   Un cheval paresseux marche sur la montagne.

5. He is swimming in a blue river.   **dans bleu nage il un fleuve**

   Il nage dans un fleuve bleu.

Avoir Besoin De: Matching

Draw lines to match the situation on the left with the sentence on the right using **avoir besoin de** (to need). One example pair has been identified for you.

1. My cousin has a big test tomorrow.
2. We have so many animals!
3. We have to cross the river without a boat!
4. My brother is lonely.
5. We want to drive to Canada!
6. My friends want fresh milk every day.
7. You look really hungry to me.
8. You want to go sailing today? You're crazy.
9. My sister wants to make money.
10. The birds are looking for a place to build a nest.

a. **Il a besoin d'un ami.**
b. **Tu as besoin du vent!**
c. **Nous avons besoin d'une grange.**
d. **Il a besoin d'étudier.**
e. **Tu as besoin de manger.**
f. **Elle a besoin de travailler.**
g. **Nous avons besoin de nager.**
h. **Ils ont besoin d'un arbre.**
i. **Nous avons besoin d'une voiture.**
j. **Ils ont besoin d'une vache.**

MEMORY : GRAMMAR : WORKSHEET : QUIZ

Nouveau Vocabulaire

Fill in the blank with the correct translation for each word.

1.	avoir besoin de, j'ai besoin de	to need, I need	6. facile	easy
2.	rouge, orange, jaune, vert, bleu, violet, blanc, noir	red, orange, yellow, green, blue, purple, white, black	7. sympathique (sympa)/gentil	nice
			8. méchant	mean
3.	intéressant	interesting	9. amusant	funny
4.	magnifique	magnificent/wonderful	10. paresseux	lazy
5.	délicieux	delicious		

Ancien Vocabulaire

Fill in the blank with the correct translation for each word.

1.	tout	everything, all	6. combien	how many? or how much?
2.	un poisson	a fish	7. un jeu	a game
3.	avoir peur de, j'ai peur de	to be afraid of, I am afraid of	8. vers	toward
4.	nager, je nage	to swim, I swim	9. s'il te plaît	please
5.	un fleuve	a river	10. un cadeau	a present, a gift

CHAPITRE 12

Avoir besoin, peur, ou faim?

This exercise uses all three different expressions we've learned with the verb **avoir** (to have). Complete the following sentences with the appropriate expression—and the right form of **avoir**, too. **Suivez l'exemple:**

Exemple:

Jonathan didn't eat anything for lunch. Now that it's dinnertime, **il _a_ _faim_**. ⚜ See p. 152 for this note.

1. My dog doesn't like to cross the street. **Il** __a__ __peur__ **des voitures.**

2. Why don't you guys want to go hiking in the woods? **Vous** __avez__ __peur__ **des ours?**

3. For Michelle's birthday party, her parents have forgotten something very important. **Ils** __ont__ __besoin__ **d'un cadeau!**

4. I don't know about you, but I haven't eaten all day. **J'**__ai__ __faim__.

5. We've got a tough test tomorrow. **Nous** __avons__ __besoin__ **d'étudier.**

6. I bet I know why you aren't coming to the pool party. **Tu** __as__ __peur__ **de nager.**

7. We are not big fans of scary movies. **Tout le temps,**[4] **nous** __avons__ __peur__!

8. Your dogs keep sniffing around my refrigerator. **Ils** __ont__ __faim__?

9. My car broke down, so I now go everywhere on foot. **J'**__ai__ __besoin__ **de marcher beaucoup!**

10. On his first day of kindergarten, Aaron is not letting his mom leave him alone with the teacher. **Il** __a__ __peur__ **de l'école.**

---

4. **Tout le temps** = "All the time." You should recognize **tout**—you learned that this word meant "everything, all" in the last **chapitre**.

MEMORY : GRAMMAR : WORKSHEET : QUIZ

Traduction

Translate the following sentences into English.

1. **Les oiseaux habitent dans un arbre magnifique.** The birds live/are living in a magnificent tree.

2. **Nous avons un chien paresseux.** We have a lazy dog.

3. **Nous mangeons un gâteau[6] délicieux.** We are eating a delicious cake.

4. **Les poissons nagent dans un lac vert.** The fish swim/are swimming in a green lake.

5. **Je joue à un jeu intéressant.** I play/am playing an interesting game.

6. **Ils ont besoin d'un chien gentil.** They need a nice dog.

7. **Elles ont peur du chat noir!** They are afraid of the black cat!

8. **Les vaches mangent dans un champ vert.** The cows eat/are eating in a green field.

9. **Vous avez faim? Vous avez besoin de manger!** You're hungry? You need to eat!

10. **Je regarde un *poisson rouge*[7] nager.** I'm looking at a red fish swim.

> ⚜ **TEACHER'S NOTE**
> The expression **poisson rouge** can be translated literally, as in "red fish," but this is also how you say "goldfish" in French!

6. The word **gâteau** means "cake."
7. In French, **poisson rouge** means "goldfish." What do the words actually mean, though?

CHAPITRE 12

MEMORY : GRAMMAR : WORKSHEET : QUIZ

Dictée!

Listen to the audio file [12_05/Tr. 79] of the **dictée** for this **chapitre**. On the lines provided, write down the three sentences you hear. You do not need to write translations for them, though it's good practice to think through what the English translation would be. You may stop and repeat the audio file several times as you're writing down the sentences.

1. **Elle a un frère intéressant.**   Translation: She has an interesting brother.

2. **Le chat a besoin d'une famille sympathique.**   Translation: The cat needs a nice family.

3. **L'oiseau mange des poissons délicieux.**   Translation: The bird is eating delicious fish.

TEACHER'S NOTE

From page 150: The following are the translations for all of the French sentences in this exercise.

Example: He is hungry.
1. He is afraid of cars.
2. You are scared of bears? *or* Are you scared of bears?
3. They need a present/gift!
4. I am hungry.
5. We need to study.
6. You are afraid of swimming.
7. We are afraid all the time! *or* (a little less naturally,) All the time, we are afraid!
8. They are hungry? *or* Are they hungry?
9. I need to walk a lot!
10. He is afraid of school. *or* He is afraid of the school.

MEMORY : GRAMMAR : WORKSHEET : QUIZ

Masculine Noun + Adjective	**Feminine Noun + Adjective**
un garçon intéressant	**une fille intéressante**
an interesting boy	an interesting girl
le lac bleu	**la mer bleue**
the blue lake	the blue sea

> **ATTENTION**
> These changes in spelling often create important changes in pronunciation. The final **e** causes us to pronounce any consonant that comes right before it. For instance, in the feminine form, we actually hear the last **t** in **intéressante**, whereas in the masculine form, we don't hear that last **t**. Listen to the audio file (13_05/Tr. 84) to hear examples from 1–3 of Adjective Agreement: Gender read aloud.

2. Adjectives that end in **-x** will change to **-se** when used with feminine nouns, as in the examples below:

Masculine Noun + Adjective	**Feminine Noun + Adjective**
un gâteau délicieux	**une glace** (ice cream) **délicieuse**
a delicious cake	a delicious ice cream
un chat heureux	**une souris heureuse**
a happy cat	a happy mouse

3. Adjectives that end in **-l**, **-t**, or **-n** may double the last consonant *and* add an extra **e**:

Masculine Noun + Adjective	**Feminine Noun + Adjective**
un gentil père	**une gentille mère**
a nice father	a nice mother
un chat mignon	**une vache mignonne**
a cute cat	a cute cow
un champ violet	**une fleur violette**
a purple field	a purple flower

MEMORY : GRAMMAR : WORKSHEET : QUIZ

4. Finally, though, you can relax. Many adjectives don't change when they are describing feminine words—they keep the same exact spelling and pronunciation—because they already have an **e** at the end in the standard form!

Masculine Noun + Adjective	*Feminine Noun + Adjective*
un jeu magnifique	**une voiture magnifique**
a wonderful game	a wonderful car
un arbre bizarre	**une maison bizarre**
a bizarre tree	a bizarre house
un jeu facile	**une école facile**
an easy game	an easy school

Adjective Agreement: Number

So far, we have seen that adjectives may change their spellings (and pronunciations!) depending on whether they are masculine or feminine, which is a shorthand way of saying whether they modify a masculine or feminine noun. The same thing happens when we are dealing with singular or plural nouns: If a noun is singular, its adjective will be singular; if a noun is plural, its adjective will also be plural. How do adjectives show that they are singular or plural? Consider the following examples—singular nouns are on the left and plural on the right, each with its corresponding adjective. Notice, also, that all of these nouns are masculine. You'll see feminine plural nouns right after.

Masculine Singular Nouns + Adjectives	*Masculine Plural Nouns + Adjectives*
l'oiseau violet	**les oiseaux violets**
the purple bird	the purple birds

> **ATTENTION**
> Don't say too much! Did we hear you pronounce the **s** on the ends of these words? No? Good, we hoped not . . .

le poisson noir	**les poissons noirs**
the black fish	the black fish

MEMORY : GRAMMAR : WORKSHEET : QUIZ

Masculine Singular Nouns + Adjectives	**Masculine Plural Nouns + Adjectives**
un chat moche	des chats moches
the ugly cat	ugly cats

Simple, huh? You just add **s**. Well . . . , most of the time.

5. There are some cases when adjectives do not change at all for plural nouns. This is true, for example, if the adjective already ends in **-x**:

Masculine Singular Nouns + Adjectives	**Masculine Plural Nouns + Adjectives**
un gâteau délicieux	des gâteaux délicieux
a delicious cake	delicious cakes

> **ATTENTION**
> Keep your guard up and don't say too much here, either! The **x** is silent in these phrases, just like the **s** above.

un garçon paresseux	des garçons paresseux
a lazy boy	lazy boys
un enfant heureux	des enfants heureux
a happy kid	happy kids

Above, you can see that adjectives ending in **-x** don't need to change when the nouns they describe are *masculine*—the nouns can be singular or plural, but the **-x** ending on the adjective remains the same. Of course, this will change once we reach *feminine* plural nouns.

What happens then? You guessed it; you need a feminine plural adjective. But don't worry! This is not so tricky: All we need to do is take the feminine singular form of the adjective and slap on an **s**.

Feminine Singular Nouns + Adjectives	**Feminine Plural Nouns + Adjectives**
la chemise violet**te**	les chemises violet**tes**[3]
the purple shirt	the purple shirts

---

3. If you want to think of it another way, we have taken the "base" adjective—the masculine singular form, **violet**—made it feminine (**violette**), and then added **s** (**violet** + **te** + **s** = **violettes**).

Feminine Singular Nouns + Adjectives

la montagne noire
the black mountain

la fille mignonne
the cute girl

la maison intéressante
the interesting house/home

la sœur paresseuse
the lazy sister

la vache heureuse
the happy cow

Feminine Plural Nouns + Adjectives

les montagnes noires
the black mountains

les filles mignonnes
the cute girls

les maisons intéressantes
the interesting houses/homes

les sœurs paresseuses
the lazy sisters

les vaches heureuses
the happy cows

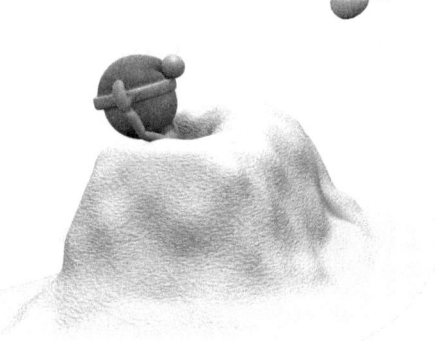

Traduction #1

You may notice that there is no exercise here . . . hmmmm . . . curious. . . . This is because the translation exercise is already built into this **chapitre**. Go back through the Grammar pages and look at the different examples of adjectives and the ways they can change their spellings. In each section you see one example of a noun + adjective combo that has been translated for you on the lines below it. You saw the following example in the first section:

un chien noir   **une vache noir*e***

a black dog   _a black cow_

Your job is to go through the rest of the examples in the Grammar pages and translate the noun + adjective combos that still have blank lines under them.

Say It Aloud!

Once again we have an opportunity to practice some of French's tricky pronunciation with this "Say it Aloud" exercise. By now you should know the drill: Translate the following sentences, and then try to pronounce each original French sentence. The lovely French voice on the audio file (13_06/Tr. 85) will read them, too, which you can use as a reference.

1. **J'ai peur des oiseaux bleus.** _I am afraid of blue birds._

2. **Vous aimez le fromage bleu?** _You like blue cheese?_

3. **Tu as un chien mignon!** _You have a cute dog!_

4. **Le père et la mère ont une fille mignonne.** _The father and the mother have a cute girl/daughter._

5. **La vache mange dans un champ vert.** _The cow eats/is eating in a green field._

MEMORY : GRAMMAR : WORKSHEET : QUIZ

6. **La vache mange des fleurs vertes.** The cow eats/is eating green flowers.

7. **Vous avez peur du chat méchant?** You're afraid of the mean cat?

8. **Non, nous avons peur de la fille méchante.** No, we're afraid of the mean girl.

9. **Nous avons un frère paresseux.** We have a lazy brother.

10. **Vous avez une sœur paresseuse?** You have a lazy sister?

Notes on Say It Aloud

Did anything surprise you about the pronunciations you heard on the audio file for this exercise? You may have noticed that the sentences came in pairs: The first sentences (1, 3, 5, 7, 9) had the "base" or "standard" masculine singular adjective, and in the second sentence of each pair (2, 4, 6, 8, 10), those adjectives changed somehow to reflect a different kind of noun.

On the lines provided, write a quick note about how the *pronunciation* changed for sentences 2, 4, 6, 8, 10:

1. What changed in sentence 2? Nothing changed in the pronunciation.

2. What changed in sentence 4? We heard the *n* sound at the end of **mignonne**.

3. What changed in sentence 6? We heard the *t* sound at the end of **vertes**.

4. What changed in sentence 8? We heard the *t* sound at the end of **méchante**.

5. What changed in sentence 10? We heard the *s* sound at the end of **paresseuse**.

CHAPITRE 13

Grammaire

Fill in or circle the correct answer.

1. A(n) _____**adjective**_____ is a word that describes a noun. It tells us the quality or the kind of noun we're talking about.

2. When we say that "adjectives must agree with their nouns," we mean that:

   a. An adjective must have the same meaning as the noun it describes.

   b. An adjective must be spelled the same as the noun it describes.

   c. An adjective must have an **e** when it describes plural nouns.

   (d.) An adjective must change its spelling to reflect the gender and number of the noun it describes.

   e. An adjective must have an **x** when it describes a plural noun, and finish with **le** or **ne** when it describes a feminine noun.

2. Imagine you had never seen the word **fromage** before. You wouldn't know if it is **le fromage** or **la fromage**. That is, you wouldn't know if it were masculine or feminine. However, if you saw the sentence: **J'aime les fromages délicieux**, you would know:

   (a.) that **fromage** is a masculine noun

   b. that **fromage** is a feminine noun

   c. that **fromage** is a stinky noun

   d. that **fromage** is an adjective

3. You are able to determine the gender of **fromage** in the sentence in question 3 because:

   a. the **s** on **fromage** tells you the gender

   b. the use of **j'aime** tells you the gender

   (c.) the ending on the adjective **délicieux** tells you the gender

   d. the word **les** tells you the gender

MEMORY : GRAMMAR : WORKSHEET : QUIZ

4. In French, you would hear _____ if someone pronounced the words **intéressant** and **intéressants** one right after the other.

   a. a small difference

   b. b. a clear difference—**intéressants** has an **s** sound at the end

   (c.) no difference

   d. an interesting difference

   e. the difference between a masculine word and a feminine word

5. Does the word **heureux** (happy) describe a singular noun or a plural noun?

   a. singular masculine noun

   (b.) we don't know

   c. plural feminine noun

   d. plural masculine noun

   e. plural masculine singular noun

6. Look at the following two columns. An English phrase is on the left, and the French translation is on the right.

a funny boy	→	**un garçon <u>amusant</u>**
a funny girl	→	**une fille <u>amusante</u>**
funny children	→	**des enfants <u>amusants</u>**
funny families	→	**des familles <u>amusantes</u>**

   The underlined French word means _____funny_____ in English. Why is it spelled differently every time in French?

   (a.) to match in number and gender the noun it describes

   b. to show just how funny each noun is

   c. to match the article (**un, une, des**)

   d. to make all of the adjectives feminine plural

MEMORY : GRAMMAR : WORKSHEET : QUIZ

Nouveau Vocabulaire

Fill in the blank with the correct translation for each word.

1. **laisser, je laisse** — to leave, I leave
2. **moche** — ugly
3. **heureux** — happy
4. **bizarre** — bizarre
5. **mignon** — cute
6. **un homme** — a man
7. **une femme** — a woman, a wife
8. **un fils** — a son
9. **une fille** — a daughter, a girl
10. **très** — very

Ancien Vocabulaire

Fill in the blank with the correct translation for each word.

1. **avoir besoin de, j'ai besoin de** — to need, I need
2. **paresseux** — lazy
3. **facile** — easy
4. **la mer** — the sea
5. **l'eau** — the water
6. **un cheval** — a horse
7. **une famille** — a family
8. **amusant** — funny
9. **manger, je mange** — to eat, I eat
10. **la plage** — the beach

MEMORY : GRAMMAR : WORKSHEET : QUIZ

Adjective Matching

The following are seven (incomplete!) sentences about Jean and Aurélie's latest friend, **Monsieur l'Oiseau**. You will see an unfinished sentence on the left and a series of two or three choices for adjectives on the right. Your job is to circle the appropriate adjective to finish the sentence. We've done one for you as an example.

L'oiseau aime le fromage . . .	bleues	bleue	**(bleu)**
1. Il chante dans les arbres . . .	magnifique	**(magnifiques)**	
2. Il habite dans la forêt . . .	vert	**(verte)**	vertes
3. L'oiseau est (is) . . .	intéressante	intéressantes	**(intéressant)**
4. Il aime la famille . . .	sympathiques	**(sympathique)**	
5. La famille habite dans une maison . . .	vertes	vert	**(verte)**
6. Elle a des enfants . . .	mignon	mignonnes	**(mignons)**

Cirque du Français

Let's imagine you want to start a circus. Luckily, your current knowledge of French will help you enormously in this task. That's because all you need to do is write a letter, in French, to the director of the major French circus company, **Le Cirque du Français**, to tell him what you need to get started. Here is a list of things you should tell him:

1. You need a magnificent tent (a tent = **une tente**).

2. You need three yellow giraffes (a giraffe = **une girafe**).

3. You need two mean bears (a bear = **un ours**).

4. You need a lot of bizarre animals.

5. You need interesting games.

6. Finally (finally = **finalement**) you need nice children in the tent!

MEMORY : GRAMMAR : WORKSHEET : QUIZ

We've started the letter for you:

Cher Monsieur le Directeur, (Dear Mr. Director,)

Je veux créer un cirque. (I want to start a circus.) J'ai besoin d'une...
tente magnifique. J'ai besoin de trois girafes jaunes. J'ai besoin de deux ours méchants. J'ai besoin de beaucoup d'animaux bizarres. J'ai besoin de jeux intéressants. Finalement, j'ai besoin des enfants sympathiques dans la tente.

Translation: I need a magnificent tent. I need three yellow giraffes. I need two mean bears. I need a lot of bizarre animals. I need interesting games. Finally, I need nice children in the tent.

Merci beaucoup. (Thank you very much.)
Cordialement, (Sincerely)

(Sign your name above)

Dictée!

Listen to the audio file [13_07/Tr. 86] of the **dictée** for this **chapitre**. On the lines provided, write down the three sentences you hear. You do not need to write translations for them, though it's good practice to think through what the English translation would be. You may stop and repeat the audio file several times as you're writing down the sentences.

1. **Nous avons un chien moche.** Translation: We have an ugly dog.

2. **Nous laissons le chien à la maison.** Translation: We leave the dog at the house.

3. **Les enfants ont peur du chien.** Translation: The children are afraid of the dog.

MEMORY : GRAMMAR : WORKSHEET : QUIZ

Before or After?

In each of the following sentences, there are two of the same adjective—one before the noun and one after the noun. That's one adjective too many! Your job has two parts:

Part 1: You must cross out the adjective that doesn't belong. How do you know which one to cross out? Well, some adjectives come *before* the noun, and other adjectives come *after* it. This **chapitre** has taught you which ones come before, and the previous two **chapitres** have shown you adjectives that come after. (Turn back to the Grammar sections of any of those chapters if you get stumped.)

Part 2: Then, on the line provided, you need to translate the sentence.

Example: **J'ai un ~~amusant~~ frère amusant.** _I have a funny brother._

1. **Jean a une petite tête ~~petite~~.** _Jean has a little head._

2. **Aurélie a une grande tête ~~grande~~.** _Aurélie has a big head._

3. **Aurélie et Jean cherchent une ~~intéressante~~ famille intéressante.** _Aurélie and Jean look/are looking for an interesting family._

4. **Ils ont des ~~noirs~~ cheveux noirs.** _They have black hair._

5. **Ils habitent dans un petit village ~~petit~~.** _They live in a little village._

6. **Aurélie cherche la famille avec les jeunes enfants ~~jeunes~~.** _Aurélie is looking for the family with the young children._

7. **Jean cherche le bon fromage ~~bon~~.** _Jean is looking for the good cheese._

8. **L'oiseau pense que la famille a des grandes oreilles ~~grandes~~.** _The bird thinks the family has big ears._

MEMORY : GRAMMAR : WORKSHEET : QUIZ

9. Il pense que la famille a des ~~verts~~ yeux verts. He thinks the family has green eyes.

Say It Aloud!

The following section contains parts of Jean and Aurélie's travel diary. Translate the sentences and then go back and pronounce each original French sentence. Keep your eyes and ears open for some of the weird pronunciation changes we predicted earlier in this **chapitre** (see the sections on Tricky Adjectives and The Curious Haves). You can hear these sentences on the audio file (14_05/Tr. 91).

1. **Nous marchons dans la forêt verte.** We walk/are walking in the green forest.

2. **Nous regardons des beaux arbres.**[9] We look/are looking at beautiful trees.

3. **Une famille intéressante habite dans le petit village près de la forêt.** An interesting family lives/is living in the little village near the forest.

4. **Les belles petites filles ont cinq, sept, et neuf ans.** The beautiful little girls are five, seven, and nine years old.

5. **Le jeune garçon a onze ans.** The young boy is eleven.

6. **Nous avons aussi onze ans! Nous espérons parler avec le jeune garçon!** We're eleven, too! We hope to speak with the young boy!

---

9. Did you notice anything strange about the pronunciation for sentence 2? You should have heard a zzz sound in between **beaux** and **arbres**. Why? Normally the **-aux** ending just sounds like "oh," right? Well, when a word *beginning with a vowel* follows a word with an **-s** or **-x** ending, the **-s** or **-x** sometimes makes a ZZZZ sound called a *liaison*. We will see many liaisons again soon; they do not happen every time there is an **-s** or an **-x** ending, but we'll learn the rules as we go. There are even a couple liaisons in sentence number 6. See if you can guess why... (Answer: The verbs **avons** and **espérons** begin with a vowel, right after a subject ending in **-s**.)

GRAMMAIRE

Fill in or circle the correct answers.

1. In French, _____ adjectives go in front of the nouns they describe.

    ⓐ some

    b. all

    c. most

    d. no

2. What is the feminine form of the masculine adjective **nouveau** (which means "new"), based on our knowledge of tricky feminine adjectives?

    a. **nouveaue**

    b. **nouveauche**

    ⓒ **nouvelle**

    d. **neweau**

3. How would you say "two eyes" in French?

    a. **deux oeils**

    b. **deux oreilles**

    c. **deux oeileux**

    ⓓ **deux yeux**

4. If someone asked you, "**Quel âge as-tu?**" In French, you would need to say:

    a. **J'aime 10.**

    b. **J'aime 10 ans.**

    c. **J'ai 10.**

    ⓓ **J'ai dix ans.**

MEMORY : GRAMMAR : WORKSHEET : QUIZ

Nouveau Vocabulaire

Fill in the blank with the correct translation for each word.

1.	**un œil/ des yeux**	an eye/eyes	6. **un nez**	a nose
2.	**un cheveu/ des cheveux**	a hair/hair	7. **bon/mauvais**	good/bad
3.	**une bouche**	a mouth	8. **grand/petit**	big/small
4.	**une oreille/ des oreilles**	an ear/ears	9. **jeune/vieux**	young/old
5.	**une tête**	a head	10. **beau** (m.) *or* **belle** (f.)	handsome *or* beautiful

Ancien Vocabulaire

Fill in the blank with the correct translation for each word.

1.	**heureux**	happy	6. **combien**	how many *or* how much
2.	**un cadeau**	a present, a gift	7. **de rien**	you're welcome
3.	**méchant**	mean	8. **un frère**	a brother
4.	**rouge**	red	9. **près (de)**	near (to), close (to)
5.	**avoir faim, j'ai faim**	to be hungry, I am hungry	10. **toujours**	always

PARTIE 3

MEMORY : GRAMMAR : WORKSHEET : QUIZ

Picture Perfect

In the space below, you will find an unfinished drawing of a person. Next to the drawing are descriptions of what the character *should* look like. As you read each sentence, draw the feature it describes on the person so that he doesn't look so . . . boring.

1. **Il a des grands yeux.**
   Translation: He has big eyes.

2. **Il a un petite nez.**
   Translation: He has a little nose.

3. **Il a des cheveux noirs.**
   Translation: He has black hair.

4. **Il a une grande bouche.**
   Translation: He has a big mouth.

5. **Il a deux petites oreilles.**
   Translation: He has two little ears.

Traduction

Traduisez (Translate) **les phrases** (the sentences) that follow.

1. **Le serpent mange le cochon; il a une grande bouche!** The snake eats/is eating the pig; it has a big mouth!

2. **Nous marchons dans une très belle forêt.** We walk/are walking in a very beautiful forest.

CHAPITRE 14 — 177

3. L'enfant étudie dans une bonne école. __The child studies/is studying in a good school.__

4. **Ton frère a un an? Tu as un jeune frère!** __Your brother is a year old? You have a young brother!__

5. J'ai un mauvais chien; il mange tout. __I have a bad dog; it eats everything.__

6. Ils ont 100 ans! Bien sûr ils ont des cheveux blancs! __They're 100 years old! Of course they have white hair!__

Dictée!

Listen to the audio file [14_06/Tr. 92] of the **dictée** for this **chapitre**. On the lines provided, write down the three sentences you hear. You do not need to write translations for them, though it's good practice to think through what the English translation would be. You may stop and repeat the audio file several times as you're writing down the sentences.

1. __Quel âge as-tu?__   Translation: How old are you?

2. __J'ai cinq ans.__   Translation: I am five years old. *or* I'm five.

3. __Tu as une grande tête!__   Translation: You have a big head!

Possessive Adjectives

Ages ago, in **chapitre** 11, we observed that in French, to express the idea of "looking for a *friend's house*," we have to say "I'm looking for the *house of a friend*": **Je cherche la maison d'un ami**. But what if you just wanted to say, "*his house*"? Or, while we're at it, what if you wanted to say "*my* house," "*your* house," or "*their* house"? In English, of course, we have the words "my," "your," "his," "her," "its," and "their." How can we say these things in French? To start, let's take the example of "my house":

ma maison

In French, **ma maison** means "my house." What is this word, **ma**? Clearly it means "my" in this expression. OK, so let's try it again. How could we say, "I'm looking for my flower"? You help by filling in the blank:

Je cherche _____ma_____ fleur.

And what about "I'm looking for my mother!"

Je cherche _____ma_____ mère!

Did you write **ma** each time? Hopefully, you did—and, hopefully, you see how easy it is to say "my house," "my car," "my mother" now. At least . . . it looks easy.

Now let's add a twist: What if we wanted to say "I'm looking for my cheese"?

Je cherche *mon* fromage.

Curious . . . How about, "I'm looking for my cat"?

Je cherche *mon* chat.

Hmm . . . Wait a minute. Where has **ma** gone? What is going on? Maybe you guessed it: *Gender* is back and at it again! The reason we said **ma** in the first three examples is because **maison**, **fleur**, and **mère** are all *feminine* words. Likewise, we said **mon** for **fromage** and **chat** because they are *masculine* words.

Now, one last trick: If you want to say, "I'm looking for my flower*s*," you don't need to worry about **mon** or **ma**. Why? Because "flowers" is a plural word, and *there is only one plural form of the possessive adjective*. In this case, it's **mes**. So, regardless of whether the noun is masculine or feminine, it is always going to be **mes** when it's plural. You can see that things become **super facile** (super easy), now! OK, **fleur** is feminine, but we don't need to worry about that since we know it is always **mes** when it's plural—**mes fleurs**. In the end, we just have: **Je cherche mes fleurs**.

MEMORY : GRAMMAR : WORKSHEET : QUIZ

We see the same pattern when we want to talk about *your* things—your house, your car, your cat. "Your house" is **ta maison**, "your flower" is **ta fleur**, and "your cat" is **ton chat**. Finally, "your flowers" follows the same old pattern and becomes **tes fleurs** in French. Here is a table to help review what you've seen so far:

English	Masculine (singular)	Feminine (singular)	Plural
my	mon (mon chat)	ma (ma fleur)	mes (mes fleurs)
your (informal, singular)	ton (ton chat)	ta (ta fleur)	tes (tes fleurs)

✱ RENVOI

Do you remember what the word "informal" means? If not, flip back to **chapitre 5**, and re-read the section on the formal "you" vs. the informal "you."

✚ REMARQUE

The transformation of **son** or **sa** to **ses** when we're dealing with plural nouns is very similar to what happens to **le** and **la**. That is, they both become **les**. It doesn't matter if it's a feminine word such as **vache** (la vache), or a masculine word such as **frère** (le frère): Both use **les**—**les vaches** and **les frères**.

What kinds of words are these—**mon, ma, ton, ta**? They are clearly not nouns—not people, places, or things. Nor are they verbs, of course. So how should we think about them? What is their function?

For one thing, when you say, "**C'est mon chat!**" (That's my cat!) you know exactly *what kind* of cat it is. It is *my* cat. The word **mon**, then, gives you more information about the noun "cat," or **chat**. Hey, that sounds a lot like a kind of word we already know: adjectives! Adjectives describe nouns—they give you more information about them. Is it a *fun* game, a *hard* game, *Fred's* game, or *my* game? The adjective tells you more information about the game. In fact, then, the words **mon, ma, ton, ta**, and a bunch of others we'll see later are all *possessive adjectives. A possessive adjective tells you who owns something—who possesses it.* And, of course, in English, the possessive adjectives are exactly that list of words we mentioned earlier: my, your, his, her, and their.

Now, take a look at the following chart. In it, we show you how to say "his" and "her(s)" (or "its") things—his cat or her cat, his flower or her flower, and his or her flowers. Study it well; we'll have a couple of questions for you on the other side.

English	Masculine Things	Feminine Things	Plural Things
his/her/its	son (son chat)	sa (sa fleur)	ses (ses fleurs)

Based on the chart, how do you suppose we'd say "his cat"? And how would we say "her cat"?

his cat = _____**son chat**_____   her cat = _____**son chat**_____

CHAPITRE 15

MEMORY : GRAMMAR : WORKSHEET : QUIZ

Traduction

Translate the following paragraph into English.

Le meunier aime beaucoup sa grande famille. Il habite avec sa femme et ses enfants. Son fils a 11 ans, et il a des cheveux noirs. Ses filles ont aussi des cheveux noirs. Ils aiment leur maison verte dans le village. Ils aiment aussi leurs animaux—beaucoup! Mais le meunier aime son âne peut-être trop : il porte son âne sur sa tête.

The miller loves his big, large family very much. He lives with his wife and his children. His son is eleven and he has black hair. His daughters also have black hair. They love their green house in the village. They also love their animals—a lot! But the miller loves his donkey perhaps too much: He carries his donkey on his head!

Grammaire

Fill in or circle the correct answers.

1. If you translated the underlined word in the following two phrases into English, would there be a difference? Why or why not?

    <u>ta</u> main   <u>tes</u> mains

    a. Yes; **ta** would be translated "her" because it is feminine and **tes** would be translated "his" because it is masculine.

    b. No; **ta** would be translated "his" because it is masculine and **tes** would be translated "his" because it is also masculine.

    c. Yes; **ta** would be translated "your" because it is singular and **tes** would be translated "you guys" because it is plural.

    (d.) No; **ta** would be translated "your," and so would **tes**, since English uses the same word in both phrases: <u>your</u> hand and <u>your</u> hands.

2. Find the correct French combination to translate "his house," and "her house":

    a. **son maison**   **sa maison**   (c.) **sa maison**   **sa maison**

    b. **son maison**   **ta maison**   d. **sa maison**   **son maison**

3. In French, you say, "**son chien**" when a *boy* owns a dog and "**sa chien**" when a girl owns a dog. Circle one: True   or   (False.)

4. Is there a difference in pronunciation between **leur chien** (their dog) and **leurs chiens** (their dogs)?

   (a.) No, **leur chien** is pronounced exactly the same way as **leurs chiens**.

   b. Yes, **leur chien** is pronounced so that you can really hear the **n** in the word **chien**.

   c. Yes, **leurs chiens** is pronounced with the first **s** very loud so that you know there is more than one dog.

   d. Yes, **leurs chiens** is pronounced with both **s**'s very clearly spoken so that we know we are dealing with a *plural* phrase.

5. Complete the following sentence: A possessive adjective is like any other adjective because it *describes* something about a noun. More specifically, a possessive adjective tells us who _____**owns**_____ or _____**possesses**_____ something.

Monsieur Lecorps[2]

Monsieur Lecorps is down to the right there. As you can see, different parts of his body have lines drawn to them. Your job is to label the parts of his body using the vocabulary you've learned over the past two **chapitres**. But before you do so, here's a strange thing (for us English speakers) to keep in mind about French: In French, we do not usually speak of parts of the body with *possessive* adjectives such as "my," "his," or "her" (**mon, ma, son, sa**, etc.). More often, we just use the definite article (**le, la, les**) even when we know exactly whose body part it is! So, when you say in English, "*My* head hurts," the French translation would be "**J'ai mal à la tête**" (literally, "I have pain in the head"). Even though there are some exceptions to this rule, it would still be wise to practice the normal pattern here and label the parts as "*the* head" or "*the* feet," etc., in French.

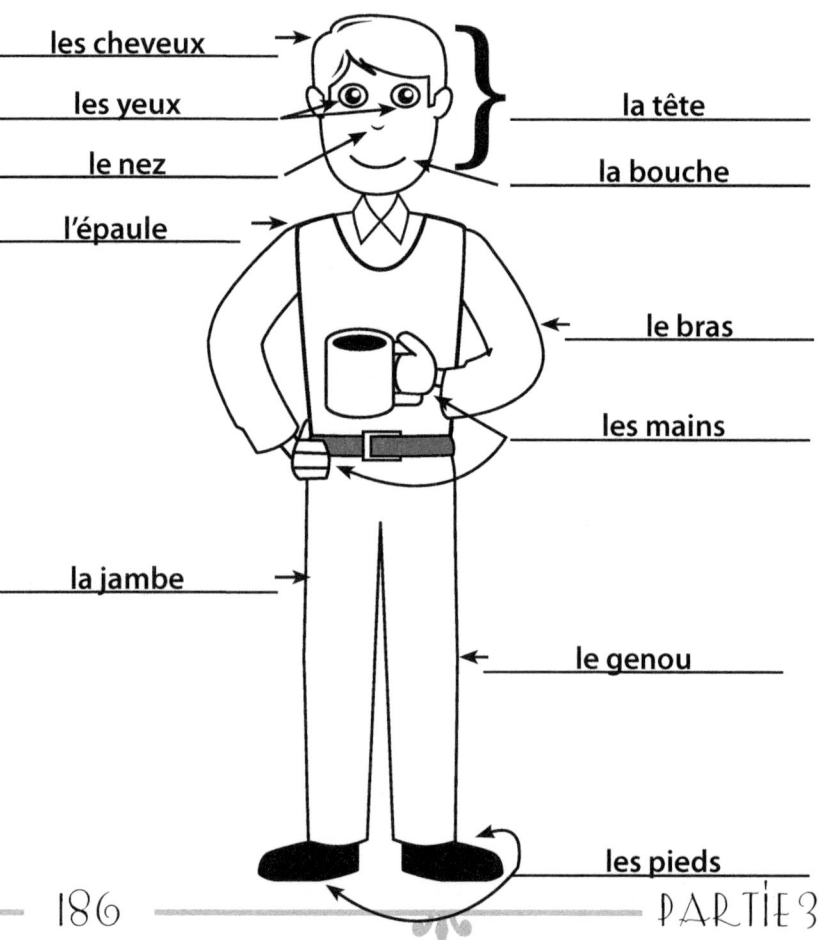

---

2. **Corps** is the French word for "body."

MEMORY : GRAMMAR : WORKSHEET : QUIZ

Nouveau Vocabulaire

Fill in the blank with the correct translation for each word.

1. **porter, je porte**	to carry, I carry	6. **le pied**	the foot
2. **la jambe**	the leg	7. **l'épaule/ les épaules**	the shoulder/shoulders
3. **la main/ les mains**	the hand/hands	8. **le dos**	the back
4. **le bras**	the arm	9. **l'âne**	the donkey
5. **le genou**	the knee	10. **trop**	too

Ancien Vocabulaire

Fill in the blank with the correct translation for each word.

1. **mauvais**	bad	6. **délicieux**	delicious
2. **le garçon**	the boy	7. **adieu**	farewell
3. **marcher, je marche**	to walk, I walk	8. **la grange**	the barn
4. **un cheveu/ des cheveux**	a hair/hair	9. **vraiment**	really
5. **derrière**	behind	10. **finir, je finis**	to finish, I finish

MEMORY : GRAMMAR : WORKSHEET : QUIZ

Chart It

Your job here is to convert these English charts into French charts. We've started the first one for you.

Anglais	Français	Anglais	Français
my dog	**mon chien**	our dog	notre chien
your dog	ton chien	your dog	**votre chien**
his dog	son chien	their dog	**leur chien**
her dog	son chien		

La Famille Des Monstres

Une famille de monstres (a monster family) is on the loose! Translate the following descriptions of them. After you're done translating their story, in the space provided draw a picture of one of them to put up all over town so that no one is taken (away) by surprise...

1. **Ils ont des yeux verts, très moches avec des cheveux bleus.** They have very ugly green eyes with blue hair.

2. **Les enfants ont peur de leur père et de sa grande tête.** The children are afraid of their father and his big head.

3. **Le père a peur de leur mère et de son nez bizarre.** The father is afraid of their mother and her bizarre nose.

4. **La mère a peur de ses enfants et de leurs grands bras et de leurs longues[3] jambes.** The mother is afraid of her children and their big arms and their long legs.

5. **Un enfant a six bras et cinq jambes.** One child has six arms and five legs.

---

3. Bet you can guess what **longue** means in English! It means long.

MEMORY : GRAMMAR : WORKSHEET : QUIZ

6. **Il nage avec ses jambes dans les lacs de la forêt.** He swims with his legs in the lakes of the forest.

7. **Il trouve des poissons avec ses six bras.** He finds fish with his six arms.

8. **Il aime manger des poissons avec ses trois grandes bouches.** He likes to eat fish with his three big mouths.

Now, draw one of the monsters in the box below!

Dictée!

Listen to the audio file [15_05/Tr. 97] of the **dictée** for this **chapitre**. On the lines provided, write down the three sentences you hear. You do not need to write translations for them, though it's good practice to think through what the English translation would be. You may stop and repeat the audio file several times as you're writing down the sentences.

1. **Leur chien a peur de marcher dans la forêt.**   Translation: Their dog is afraid of walking in the forest.
2. **Il préfère rester dans sa maison.**   Translation: He prefers to stay in his house.
3. **Je mange ton fromage.**   Translation: I eat/I'm eating your cheese.

REVIEW

CHAPITRE 16 SEIZE

This unit was **très longue** (very long)! You have fifty new vocabulary words to remember this time around. You know the drill: Put a check mark next to any word that you might have forgotten, note it on your list of words to master, and **révisez, révisez, révisez** (review, review, review)!

	French	English		French	English
☐	avoir peur de, j'ai peur de	to be afraid of, I'm afraid of	☐	intéressant	interesting
☐	nager, je nage	to swim, I swim	☐	magnifique	magnificent, wonderful
☐	la mer	the sea	☐	délicieux	delicious
☐	le fleuve	the river	☐	facile	easy
☐	le lac	the lake	☐	sympathique (sympa)/ gentil	nice
☐	la plage	the beach	☐	méchant	mean
☐	le poisson	the fish	☐	amusant	funny
☐	l'eau	the water	☐	paresseux	lazy
☐	près (de)	near (to), close (to)	☐	laisser, je laisse	to leave, I leave
☐	tout	everything, all	☐	moche	ugly
☐	avoir besoin de, j'ai besoin de	to need, I need	☐	heureux	happy
			☐	bizarre	bizarre
☐	rouge, orange, jaune, vert, bleu, violet, blanc, noir	red, orange, yellow, green, blue, purple, white, black	☐	mignon	cute
			☐	un homme	a man
			☐	une femme	a woman, a wife

Review

French	English	French	English
☐ un fils	a son	☐ beau (m.) or belle (f.)	handsome or beautiful
☐ une fille	a daughter, a girl	☐ porter, je porte	to carry, I carry
☐ très	very	☐ la jambe	the leg
☐ un œil/ des yeux	an eye/eyes	☐ la main/ les mains	the hand/hands
☐ un cheveu/ des cheveux	a hair/hair	☐ le bras	the arm
☐ une bouche	a mouth	☐ le genou	the knee
☐ une oreille/ des oreilles	an ear/ears	☐ le pied	the foot
☐ une tête	a head	☐ l'épaule/ les épaules	the shoulder/shoulders
☐ un nez	a nose	☐ le dos	the back
☐ bon/mauvais	good/bad	☐ l'âne	the donkey
☐ grand/petit	big/small	☐ trop	too
☐ jeune/vieux	young/old		

My List of Words to Master

So that you can easily review the words you are having difficulty remembering, write them down on the lines provided below.

1. _____
2. _____
3. _____
4. _____
5. _____

6. _____
7. _____
8. _____
9. _____
10. _____

GRAMMAIRE

De + *Articles* (**Chapitre** *11*)

Surely you remember the exploits of the daring **de** from **chapitre** 11. How does the preposition **de** combine with words around it? Here is the chart one more time—study it well before moving on to the exercise.

Article	Article + de	Exemples en français
la	**de + la** → **de la** (This combination doesn't change!)	**J'habite près *de la* montagne.** (I live near the mountain.)
le	**de + le** → **du**	**Elle marche près *du* château.** (She is walking near the castle.)
les	**de + les** → **des**	**Nous cherchons le champ *des* chevaux.** (We are looking for the horses' field.)
une	**de + une** → **d'une**	**Il habite près *d'une* école.** (He lives near a school.)
un	**de + un** → **d'un**	**La girafe mange près *d'un* arbre.** (The giraffe is eating near a tree.)

When the word **de** meets the following words, what happens?

1. **de + la maison** = _de la maison_

2. **de + un chien** = _d'un chien_

3. **de + les frères** = _des frères_

4. **de + l'école** = _de l'école_

5. **de + une famille** = _d'une famille_

6. **de + le vent** = _du vent_

REVIEW

Adjectives (**Chapitres** 12–14)

Before launching into these exercises, let us review a few golden rules of adjectives. First of all, what is an adjective? You complete the phrase: An *adjective* is a word that _____describes_____ a _____noun_____.

We've said that in French, adjectives such as "big, large" (**grand**) or "white" (**blanc**) do not behave as English adjectives do. Here are the golden rules for working with French adjectives—**les adjectifs**!

Golden Rules of French Adjectives	
1. Adjectives *usually* come *after* nouns, not before.	Example: **J'aime l'oiseau *bleu*.**
2. Adjectives must *agree* with their nouns in *number* (singular or plural).	Example: **J'aime les oiseaux *bleus*.**
3. Adjectives must *agree* with their nouns in *gender* (masculine or feminine).	Example: **J'aime la fille *intéressante*.** or **J'aime les voitures *noires*.** [The last sentence shows agreement with gender—the single underlined **e**—as well as agreement with number—the double underlined **s**.]
4. Some adjectives come before the noun. You have learned the following words that obey the BAGS (beauty, age, goodness, size) rule: **bon, mauvais, grand, jeune, vieux, petit, beau**.	Example: **J'aime la *petite* maison.**

Qu'est-ce que tu préfères?

The question above means, "What do you prefer?" You will learn more about how to ask questions such as that one in *French for Children Primer B*. For now, you don't need to ask the questions, you just need to answer them. The following are a series of questions asking you which thing you'd prefer in a few different situations. Though opinions could differ, there is probably only one "correct" answer for each question.

1. You have to pick a partner with whom you will work in school. **Qu'est-ce que tu préfères?**

    a. **un garçon méchant**   a mean boy

    b. **un garçon paresseux**   a lazy boy

    ⓒ **un garçon gentil**   a nice boy

CHAPITRE 16 — 195

REVIEW

2. You need to find a dog to guard your house. **Qu'est-ce que tu préfères?**

    a. **un chien amusant**   a funny dog

    (b.) **un chien méchant**   a mean dog

    c. **un chien paresseux**   a lazy dog

3. You've just won a new car! **Qu'est-ce que tu préfères?**

    (a.) **une bonne voiture**   a good car

    b. **une mauvaise voiture**   a bad car

    c. **une voiture moche**   an ugly car

Find the Right Combo

In each of the following questions, there is one adjective + noun combination that is correct, along with three phony combinations. Use your knowledge of gender, number, and adjective to pick out the right combination. Then, translate that combination on the line provided.

Exemple: **Ils regardent le . . .**

a. **chat noires**   b. **chat noire**   (c.) **chat noir**   d. **chat noirs**

Translation: _black cat_

1. **J'aime parler avec des . . .**   I like/love talking/speaking with . . .

    a. **amis sympathique**   b. **ami sympathiques**   (c.) **amis sympathiques**

    d. **ami sympathique**

    Translation: _nice friends_

2. **Vous avez des . . .**   You have . . .

    a. **cheveux blanches**   b. **cheveux blanc**   (c.) **cheveux blancs**   d. **cheveux blanche**

    Translation: _white hair_

3. **Elle mange un . . .**   She eats/is eating a . . .

    (a.) **fromage délicieux**   b. **fromages délicieux**   c. **fromage délicieuse**

    d. **fromage délicieuses**

    Translation: _delicious cheese_

REVIEW

4. **Nous cherchons une . . .**   We are look for/are looking for a . . .

   a. **grand voiture**   b. **voiture grande**   c. **voiture grand**   ⓓ **grande voiture**

   Translation: _big car_

5. **Elles nagent dans un . . .**   They swim/are swimming in a . . .

   ⓐ **magnifique fleuve**   b. **fleuve magnifique**   c. **magnifiques fleuve**

   d. **fleuve magnifiques**

   Translation: _magnificent river_

Possessive Adjectives (Chapitre 15)

Conjugation and Possessives

This exercise is a double whammy that asks you to dust off your verb conjugations *and* use the correct possessive adjective to match the subject of the sentence. So, first you'll need to conjugate the verb that you see in parentheses in each sentence. Then, in the blank that's labeled *PA* (for *possessive adjective*), you should write one of the possessive adjectives you learned in **chapitre 15**: **mon, ma, mes, son, sa, ses, votre**, etc. We've done one for you:

Example : **Le garçon _a_ (avoir) peur de _son_ frère.**
                                                    PA

1. **Je ___marche___ (marcher) vers ___mon___ école.**
                                                     PA
   I walk/am walking toward my school.

2. **La vache ___aime___ (aimer) habiter dans ___sa___ grange.**
                                                              PA
   The cow loves/likes living in her barn.

3. **Les enfants ___regardent___ (regarder) ___leur___ mère.**
                                                           PA
   The children look at/are looking at their mother.

4. **Vous ___cherchez___ (chercher) ___votre___ maison?**
                                                      PA
   You look/are looking for your house/home?

5. **Nous ___aimons___ (aimer) beaucoup ___nos___ chiens.**
                                                        PA
   We like/love our dogs a lot.

6. **Elle ___a___ (avoir) sept ans, et ___ses___ amis ont huit ans.**
                                                                PA
   She is seven years old and her friends are eight years old.

CHAPITRE 16

CHAPITRE 17 DIX-SEPT

END-OF-BOOK REVIEW

Félicitations! (Congratulations!) You've made it! Here we are at the last chapter, **le dernier chapitre**, to take some time to review all that you've learned. This end-of-book review **chapitre** is organized according to three units, or **parties**, of this book:

- **Partie** 1: Subjects and Present-Tense Verbs
- **Partie** 2: Articles and Plural Nouns
- **Partie** 3: The Preposition **de** and Adjectives

Plus, we'll have a final vocabulary review at the end just to make sure all of those new words are properly tucked away in the French-speaking corner of your brain.

Partie 1: Subjects and Present-Tense Verbs

1. Fill in the following chart. Make sure you write the correct subject and the correct conjugation. The first box has been done for you as an example.

Marcher *(to walk)*

Person	Singular	Plural
1st Person	**je marche** (I walk)	nous marchons (we walk)
2nd Person	tu marches (you walk)	vous marchez (you walk)
3rd Person	il/elle marche (he/she/it walks)	ils/elles marchent (they walk)

END-OF-BOOK REVIEW

2. Choose the correct subject pronoun to replace the subjects (in parentheses) in the following sentences. Then, translate the sentences (with the subject pronouns) into English. An example has been provided.

   Exemple: (Mon frère et moi) <u>Nous</u> **aimons la ville.**
   Translation: <u>We like the city.</u>

   a. **(Philippe)** _____<u>Il</u>_____ **cherche la voiture.**

   Translation: <u>He looks/is looking for the car.</u>

   b. **(Toi)** _____<u>Tu</u>_____ **penses que la voiture est là-bas?**

   Translation: <u>You think that the car is over there?</u>

   c. **(Toi et ton ami)** _____<u>Vous</u>_____ **avez les cheveux noirs.**

   Translation: <u>You have black hair.</u>

   d. **(Elisabeth)** _____<u>Elle</u>_____ **a peur de la forêt.**

   Translation: <u>She is afraid of the forest.</u>

   e. **(Elisabeth et sa mère)** _____<u>Elles</u>_____ **préfèrent la plage.**

   Translation: <u>They prefer the beach.</u>

   f. **(Jean et Aurélie)** _____<u>Ils</u>_____ **parlent avec le cheval.**

   Translation: <u>They're talking with the horse.</u>

Partie 2: Articles and Plural Nouns

1. Circle the correct answer. If you pronounced the words **serpent** and **serpents** in French, would you hear a difference?

   a. Yes, but there is not a very big difference.

   (b.) No, there is no difference at all.

   c. Yes, whenever you add letters to a word in French, you change the sound.

   d. Yes, it would be just like the difference between "cent" and "cents" in English.

END-OF-BOOK REVIEW

2. Circle the correct answer. To say, "The woman needs four horses" in French, you would say:

   a. **La femme a besoin de quatre chevals.**

   b. **La femme a besoin de quatre cheval.**

   c. **La femme a besoin de quatre chevaux.** ⟵ (circled)

   d. **La femme a besoin de quatre chevauls.**

3. Each of the following boxes contains a description of one of the seven French articles. Draw lines to link the descriptions to their matching articles.

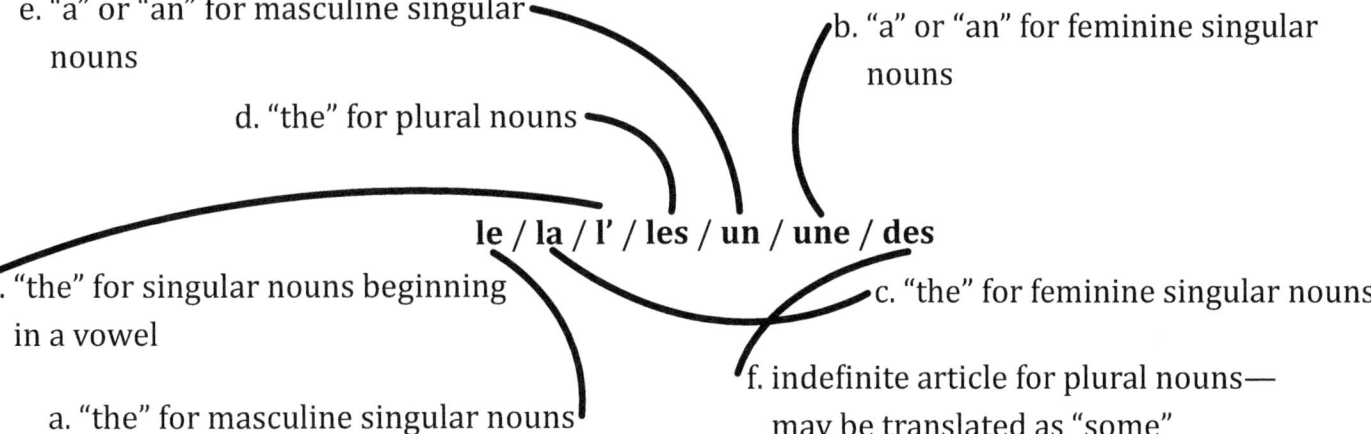

e. "a" or "an" for masculine singular nouns

b. "a" or "an" for feminine singular nouns

d. "the" for plural nouns

le / la / l' / les / un / une / des

g. "the" for singular nouns beginning in a vowel

c. "the" for feminine singular nouns

a. "the" for masculine singular nouns

f. indefinite article for plural nouns—may be translated as "some"

4. In each of the following boxes, there is a word on the left, and the plural form of that word on the right. However, some of the plural forms are not quite as they should be. Find and cross out the problem plurals. Then, write the correct form on the blank provided.

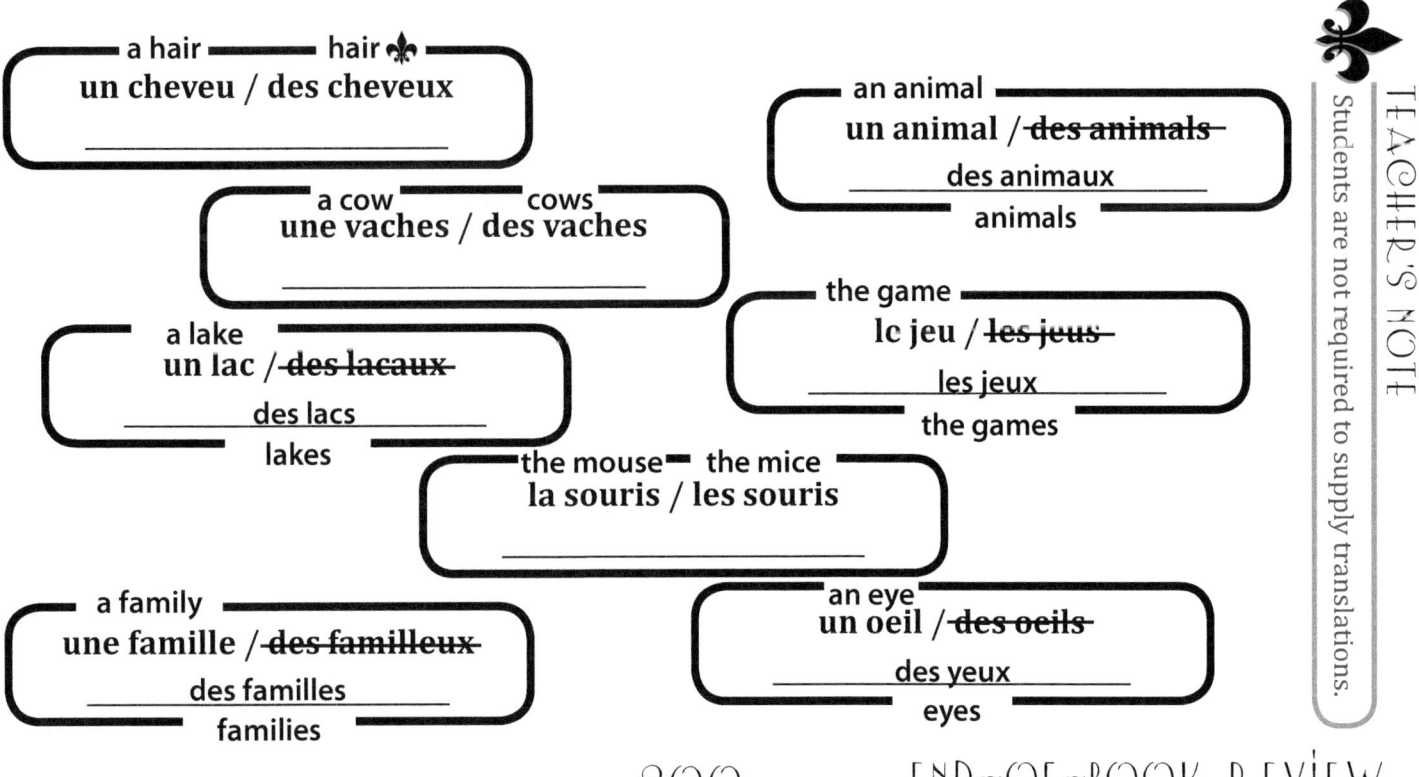

a hair — hair ⚜
un cheveu / des cheveux

a cow — cows
une vaches / des vaches

an animal
un animal / ~~des animals~~
___des animaux___
animals

a lake
un lac / ~~des lacaux~~
___des lacs___
lakes

the game
le jeu / ~~les jeus~~
___les jeux___
the games

the mouse — the mice
la souris / les souris

a family
une famille / ~~des familleux~~
___des familles___
families

an eye
un oeil / ~~des oeils~~
___des yeux___
eyes

Teacher's Note: Students are not required to supply translations.

200

END-OF-BOOK REVIEW

Partie 3: The Preposition de and Adjectives

1. To complete the following sentences, circle the correct form of the preposition **de**. You may need to check the gender of a word to be sure. (See the glossary in the back of the book.) If you're a little rusty on how **de** combines with other words, flip back to **chapitre** 11.

   a. **Les chevaux ont peur** _____ **serpent.**   The horses are afraid of the snake.

   (des / de la /(**du**))

   b. **Ils ont besoin** _____ **carte.**   They need a map.

   (des / du /(**d'une**))

   c. **Jean, Aurélie, et Thibault marchent près** _____ **forêt.**   Jean, Aurélie, and Thibault walk/are walking near the forest.

   (des / de /(**de la**))

   d. **Ils habitent loin** _____ **ville.**   They live far from the city.

   (de / du /(**de la**))

   e. **Ils regardent un serpent à côté** _____ **arbres.**   They are looking at a snake next to the trees.

   de / d'un /(**des**))

   f. **Le serpent préfère habiter loin** _____ **zoo.**   The snake prefers to live far from the zoo.

   (des / de la /(**du**))

2. You know by now that adjectives—words such as **grand** (big), **jaune** (yellow), or **paresseux** (lazy)—are words used to describe nouns. You learned that, in French, adjectives must *agree* with their nouns in gender and number. In the following exercise, use the adjective provided to complete *all four* blanks in each sentence, changing the spelling of the adjective to agree with the noun it describes where necessary.

   Observations from the Picky Heron   Adjective: **noir** (black)
   Exemple: Dans la forêt _noire_ avec des arbres _noirs_ tu regardes les poissons _noirs_ dans le lac _noir_. In the black forest, with black trees, you are looking at the black fish (plural) in the black lake.

   Thibault's Family: Adjective: **petit** (small)
   Ils habitent dans une _____petite_____ maison verte dans un _____petit_____ village, à côté des _____petits_____ champs avec des _____petites_____ vaches.   They live in a small house in a small village next to small fields with small cows.

END-OF-BOOK REVIEW

3. You probably remember that some adjectives come *before* the nouns they describe. In the following sentences, circle the correct placement of the adjective (before or after the noun).

   a. **Nous avons un** _____ **chien** _____. We have a lazy dog.

   paresseux   (paresseux)

   b. **Ils habitent dans une** _____ **maison** _____. They live in a big house.

   (grande)   grande

   c. **J'ai un** _____ **frère** _____. I have an interesting brother.

   intéressant   (intéressant)

   d. **Nous aimons des** _____ **devoirs** _____. We like easy homework.

   faciles   (faciles)

VOCABULARY REVIEW

Try your hand at this final test of the vocabulary you've learned in this book. You should be able to score at least 75 percent on this test (though we hope it will be as close to 100 percent as possible!). If you don't score at least 75 percent, keep reviewing your vocabulary, and you will get there eventually, with practice, as you continue your studies. The numbers after each word tell you from which chapter the word comes.

French	English	French	English
1. étudier, j'étudie (1)	to study, I study	6. pour (2)	for
2. parler, je parle (1)	to speak, I speak	7. réussir, je réussis (3)	to succeed, I succeed
3. à (1)	to, at	8. rester, je reste (3)	to stay, I stay
4. travailler, je travaille (2)	to work, I work	9. ici (4)	here
5. la forêt (2)	the forest	10. habiter, j'habite (4)	to live, I live

END-OF-BOOK REVIEW

French	English	French	English
11. dans (4)	in	28. paresseux (12)	lazy
12. jouer, je joue (6)	to play, I play	29. laisser, je laisse (13)	to leave, I leave
13. le renard (6)	the fox	30. heureux (13)	happy
14. à côté de (6)	next to	31. mignon (13)	cute
15. tomber, je tombe (7)	to fall, I fall	32. un œil/des yeux (14)	an eye/eyes
16. la fleur (7)	the flower	33. une oreille/des oreilles (14)	an ear/ears
17. loin (de) (7)	far (from)	34. jeune/vieux (14)	young/old
18. avoir, j'ai (8)	to have, I have	35. bon/mauvais (14)	good/bad
19. un enfant (8)	a child	36. porter, je porte (15)	to carry, I carry
20. une sœur (8)	a sister	37. la main/les mains (15)	the hand/hands
21. un ami (9)	a friend		
22. mais (9)	but		
23. avoir peur de, j'ai peur de (11)	to be afraid of, I'm afraid of		
24. près (de) (11)	near (to)		
25. tout (11)	everything, all		
26. facile (12)	easy		
27. méchant (12)	mean		

CHAPITRE 17 — 203

Appendix A: Dialogue Translations

Aurélie. **Bonsoir!** (Good evening!)

Jean. H-h-hi!

Aurélie. **Je m'appelle Aurélie.** (My name is Aurélie.)

Le Chat. **Je m'appelle Monsieur le Chat. Et comment t'appelles-tu?** (My name is Mr. Cat. And what's your name?)

Jean. **Je m'appelle Jean. Enchanté.** (My name is Jean. Nice to meet you.)

Le Chat. **Enchanté. Alors!** (Nice to meet you. So!) Are you lost?

Jean. **Un peur** (A fear)—I mean **un peu** (a little). ⚜

Aurélie. **Beaucoup, Jean! Nous cherchons le zoo.** (A lot, Jean! We're looking for the zoo.)

Le Chat. **Ah, vous cherchez le zoo?** (Ah, you're looking for the zoo?)

Jean, *gathering courage.* Yes, we are. And what are you doing in that tree, **Monsieur le Chat** (Mr. Cat)?

Aurélie. **Tu travailles dans l'arbre?** (Do you work in the tree?)

Le Chat. **Comment? Non, non!** (Excuse me!? No, no!) I do not *work* in the tree. I'm *hiding* in it—from dogs. Hunting dogs. They're in the forest, you know.

Aurélie. **Un chien? Dans la forêt!?** (A dog? In the forest!?)

Le Chat. Not just *one* dog . . . dozens. And yes, they're here in the forest—you'd better be careful. **Attention!** (Watch out!) Anyway, the fastest way back to town is to cross the river at the base of the mountain . . . but it's a long ways off.

Aurélie. **Ah non! Je reste. Je reste ici. Je préfère rester ici!** (Oh no! I'm staying. I'm staying here. I prefer to stay here!)

Jean. Absolutely not, Aurélie! If you stay here, you're dead meat. We've got to keep going! **Allons-y!** (Let's go!)

Le Chat. **Chhhhuuuuuut!** (Shhhhhhhhh!) You shouldn't be talking so loudly. And yes, you should be on your way. **J'espère que vous réussissez! J'espère que vous trouvez le zoo. Au revoir!** (I hope you succeed! I hope you find the zoo. Good-bye!)

Aurélie. **Oui, j'espère que nous trouvons le zoo. Au revoir, Monsieur le Chat!** (Yes, I hope we find the zoo. Good-bye, Mr. Cat!)

> ## Teacher's Note
>
> ⚜ A similar joke in English would be, "A bite—I mean a bit." You can use this opportunity to explain to your students that jokes are often very difficult to translate, especially when the humor comes from the similarity of the sounds of different words. Words that sound very similar (or are the same) in one language may be very different from each other in another language.

Appendix B: Chant Translations

Chapitre 1

Je parle: *I speak, I am speaking*

Chant	Translation
Je parle, je parle, chut, chut, chut!	I'm speaking, I'm speaking, shhh, shhh, shhh!

Chapitre 2

Parler: *to speak/talk*

> **TEACHER'S NOTE**
> The verb **parler** could also be translated as "to talk" in this chant.

Chant	Translation
Parler! Je parle, tu parles, il/elle parle. Parler! Nous parlons, vous parlez, ils/elles parlent. Parler!	To speak! I speak, you speak, he/she speaks. To speak! We speak, you speak, they speak. To speak!

Chapitre 3

> **TEACHER'S NOTE**
> Note: The difference between the two forms of "they" is more fully explained in **chapitre** 7.

Finir: *to finish*

Chant	Translation
Je finis, tu finis, il finit, and **elle finit**, **nous finissons, vous finissez, ils finissent,** and **elles finissent**.	I finish, you finish, he finishes, and she finishes, we finish, you finish, they finish, and they finish.

Chapitre 4

Subject Pronouns

Person	Singular	Plural
1st Person	**je** (I)	**nous** (we)
2nd Person	**tu** (you)	**vous** (you all)
3rd Person	**il/elle** (he/she/it)	**ils/elles** (they)

Notes

Why study Latin?

Dorothy Sayers points out that when you study Latin, you are doing advanced study in several subjects simultaneously. The following are some of those other subjects studied in and through Latin as well as some of the benefits of studying Latin:

- Professions steeped in Latin vocabulary: Law, medicine, science, music, art, philosophy, and theology derive many of their terms and phrases from Latin.

- Romance languages: Spanish, French, Italian, Portuguese, and Romanian are all forms of Latin.

- Educational virtues: The study of Latin requires concentration, analysis, and puzzle solving that develop a student as a student. It also helps gifted students to slow down and attend!

- English vocabulary: 50% of all English words and 90% of all polysyllabic words come from Latin.

- English grammar: Latin grammar is ideal for shedding light on the way all languages work.

- Writing/reading: An increased vocabulary and understanding of grammar enable students to write and read with greater ease and clarity.

- Pleasure: Deciphering the "secret code" of Latin and reading great authors in their own tongue are pleasures that can last a lifetime!

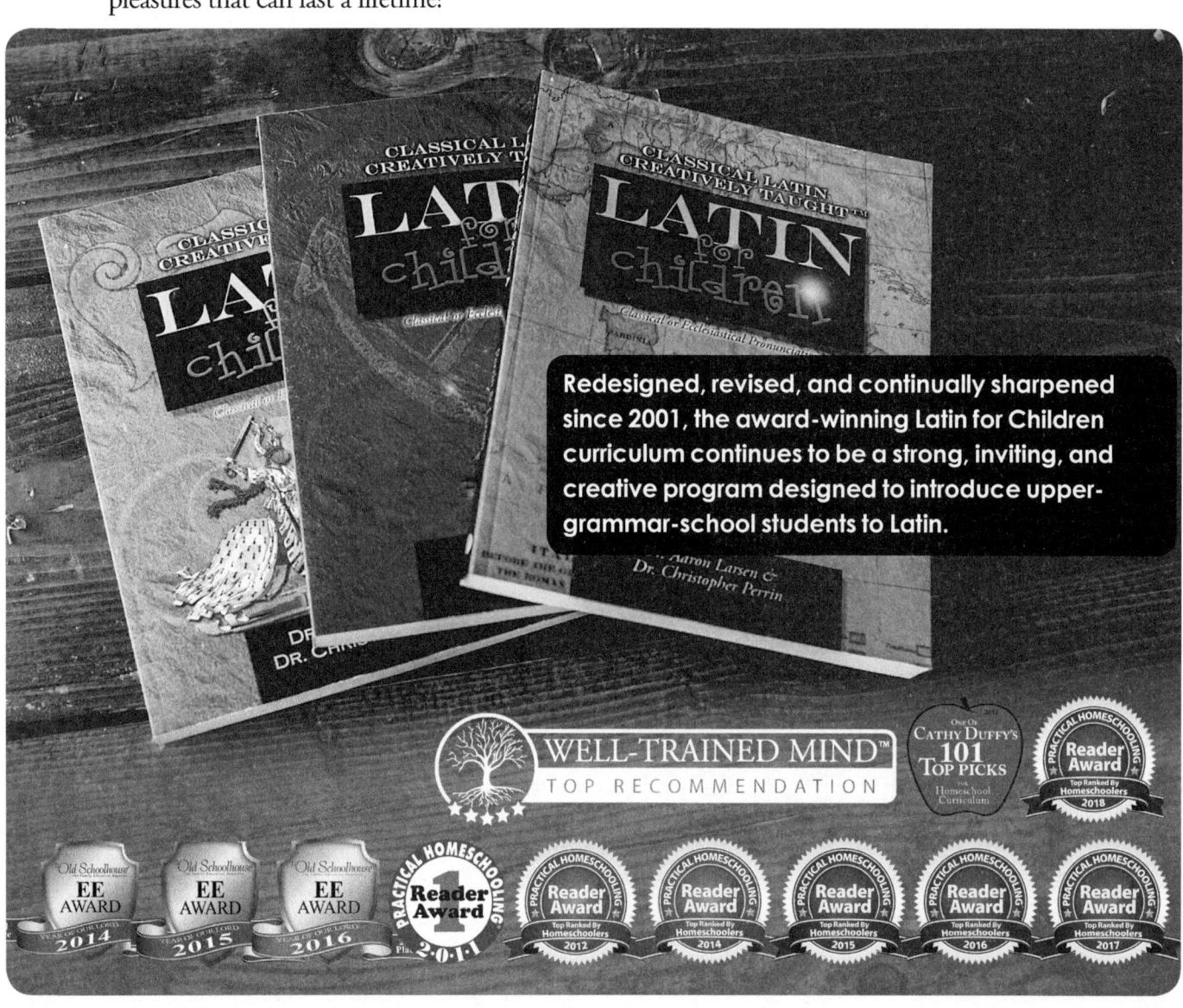

Redesigned, revised, and continually sharpened since 2001, the award-winning Latin for Children curriculum continues to be a strong, inviting, and creative program designed to introduce upper-grammar-school students to Latin.

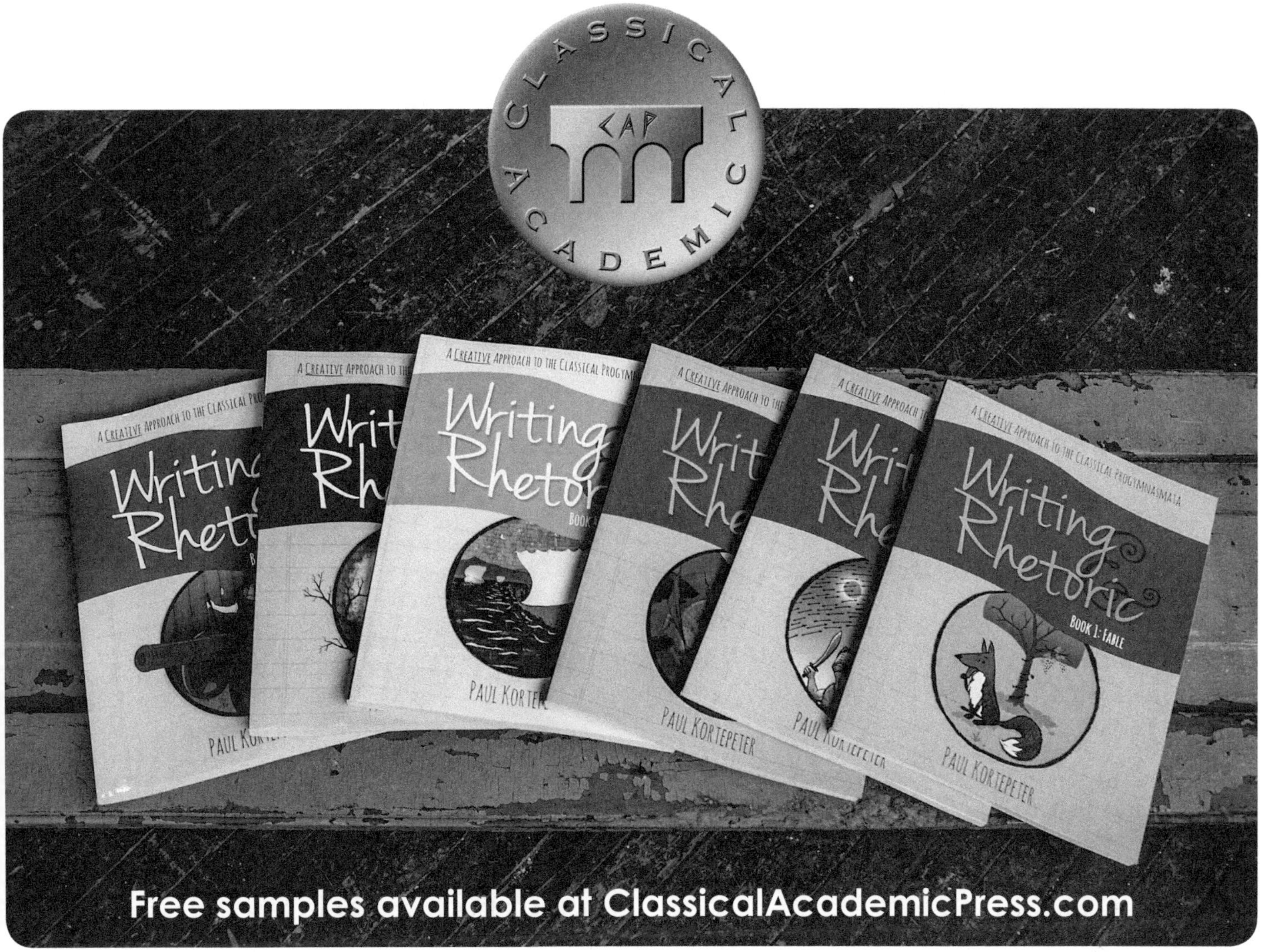

Free samples available at ClassicalAcademicPress.com

"My students love these books. The stories are wonderful and engaging and we have had so much fun with it. They are making great progress and have moved from dreading their writing assignments to eagerly anticipating them each week."
—Teren, Cottage School Director

"Classical Academic Press has successfully created a truly classical writing program for the modern student." —Sarah Mackenzie, *Read-Aloud Revival*

"This has been our most successful writing program ever!"
—Elissa, home educator

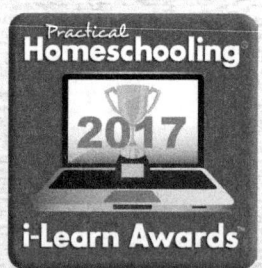

Live, Online Learning!

Live, online courses for grades 3–12 that are classical and restful, cultivating a deep engagement with learning.

SCHOLÉ ACADEMY
CLASSICAL ACADEMIC PRESS

ScholeAcademy.com